Nearly ninety

By the same author

FIFTY YEARS YOUNG: THE STORY OF AN ÓIGE
SLANE: SLANE TOWN TRAIL: NEWGRANGE.

Acknowledgments

I wish to express my thanks to the Lilliput Press and Andrée Sheehy-Skeffington for permission to quote from her biography, *Skeff: a Life of Owen Sheehy-Skeffington*; to D. R. O'Connor Lysaght for permission to quote from his writings as indicated in my chapter on 'An Irish Trotskyist'; and above all to Fiachra and Brian for their great help in processing and editing my typescript, for reference to sources and for much appreciated advice.

NEARLY NINETY

REMINISCENCES

Chalmers (Terry) Trench

The Hannon Press

For Fiachra, Brian, Beatrice and Patrick
and in memory of their mother

Contents

NEARLY NINETY
A Hannon Book

ISBN O 9516472 4 5

Published in Ireland by The Hannon Press,
Ballivor, Co. Meath

Designed and Typeset by
Steven Hope Design
21 Shenick Grove, Skerries, Co. Dublin

Printed in Dublin by ColourBooks Ltd.,
105 Baldoyle Industrial Estate, Baldoyle, Dublin 13.

Cover painting by Michael O'Dea

I

Galway-Blessington-Dublin

I have always been inclined to stress the fact that I was born in Galway because, although I was only two years old when we left there, it is mainly with Galway that the Trench family was associated from the mid-17th century and into the 20th century. Admittedly, the association was with Ballinasloe and Woodlawn, at the eastern end of the county Galway, some forty miles east of Galway city, and it was more or less fortuitous that I, along with my brother, Patrick (b. 1905) and sisters, Sheela (b. 1907) and Shamrock (b. 1908), was born in that city. My birth was on 27 November 1909. It was fortuitous in that it arose from the fact simply that my father, Wilbraham FitzJohn Trench, held a chair in the Queen's College, Galway, from 1899. He had not previously lived in Galway. Shamrock was the pet-name by which the younger of my two sisters was best known in Ireland. Her official names included Netta, by which she was known in her childhood and early adolescence, and Jean, by which she was known once she moved to England.

At the age of twenty-six, WFT was appointed Professor of History, English Literature and Mental Science, without having occupied any lesser teaching post anywhere. This curious triple chair might be thought to have been a device to enable the college to fill three chairs, which it was statutorily obliged to do, for the price of one, but in fact the triple title was laid down in the statutes issued under the charter of 1846.

The author aged 9 months, with his sisters Sheela and Shamrock on the switchback at Winscales, nr. Workington, Aug. 1920

The author aged 2 years, 9 months, Aug. 1912

Photo: Lafayette, Dublin

The author in 1916, aged 6 years, 8 months

Photo: Lafayette, Dublin

Under the heading of Mental Science, my father originally gave an occasional lecture in Logic, but was soon able to confine himself to the English Literature part of his professorship. He was not required to lecture in History, but he had a very keen sense of history. He was very conscious and wary of the common habit of interpreting history in a particular way to suit the prejudices of the interpreter.

In Galway, WFT was very anxious to associate himself with any organization that seemed to him to be working for the common good. This included the campaign to promote the sale of Irish goods. As a founder member of the Galway Industrial Development Association in 1906 and its president from 1907 to 1910, he was heavily involved in the organizing of the Fourth All-Ireland Industrial Conference and Exhibition, held in Galway in 1908. In this connection, a medal was struck for presentation to the foreign delegates, who came from eleven different countries. The medal was designed by (Sir) Hugh Lane, a Governor and Guardian of the National Gallery of Ireland and a great benefactor to that gallery and to the Municipal Gallery of Modern Art, but not known as a designer. There is a specimen of the medal in Galway City Museum, presented by me in 1978 through the Friends of the National Collections of Ireland. It was the subject of articles of mine in the *Irish Independent* of 25 March 1975 and *Irish Numismatics,* no. 49, January–February 1976.

My father was concerned to take some action to enable the small producers around Loch Corrib to bring their produce into market in Galway. He decided that the way to do this was to run a steamer on Loch Corrib, specifically for them rather than for tourists.

He persuaded the Congested Districts Board to make piers available, where the steamer could tie up, and to promise a grant of £100 per annum for the service. He knew little about boats and I suppose that he depended on the advice of P. Walsh, of Wood Quay, Galway, who became captain of the steamer which my father bought in Enniskillen. Her name was *Widgeon,* but my father renamed her *Clíodhna,* after the legendary figure who gave her name to one of the three great waves of Ireland. There being no south-westerly outlet from Loch Erne, *Clíodhna* made an epic 480-mile voyage by river, canel and open sea, into Loch Corrib, details of which I have given in *Inland Waterways News* (vol. 18, no. 2, April 1991). My father joined her for the journey from Dublin by the Grand Canal and the River Shannon to Limerick.

The service was not adequately supported by the country people and was never a success and *Clíodhna* was sold in 1908 to the Great Southern and Western Railway Company and taken down to Parknasilla, Co. Kerry, where she sank at anchor on the day after her arrival.

My father lost some of his limited means in this venture and in other ventures to promote Irish industry, such as the Galway Granite Company, which supplied the stone for the Parnell monument in O'Connell Street, Dublin, and then went into liquidation. But he recovered all his losses in later years by an investment in the Dublin Steam Trawling Company, which supplied us with a whole turbot for the family dinner on one occasion when we were living at 6 Clyde Road.

Amongst his other activities, WFT was a founder member in 1900 of the Galway Archaeological and Historical Society, its first (joint) Honorary Secretary and editor of the first five volumes of its Journal, 1900–1908. He had an interest in the Irish language as representing one of the many cultural strands to which we are heirs, though this was not the common view of people of his generation and his upbringing in Dublin and Belfast. In the 1920s and 1930s he never adopted the general antagonism to the language which was engendered by the 'compulsory Irish' policy of the Irish Free State.

While I was at school in England, I received some official communication from Ireland, probably relating to my request for a passport in 1926. In accordance with the normal practice, the text of the letter was in English, but it opened with *A chara* and closed with *Mise, le meas*. I had not met this before, and I wrote to my father for an explanation. He not only told me that these words meant 'Friend' and 'I am, with respect', but in order to put it in a historical context he said that an Irish chieftain or nobleman when writing Gaelic

The Galway Medal, designed at W.F. Trench's request by (Sir) Hugh Lane for presentation to the foreign delegates at the All-Ireland Industrial Conference and Exhibition in Galway, 1908. The medal is bronze and enamel and measures 55 by 45 mm.

The obverse is a design suggested by the Arms of Ireland and shows on a field in light blue enamel, a golden harp between three shamrocks in green enamel, all surrounded in low relief by a rendering in Irish of the words: All Ireland Industrial Conference.

The reverse design, suggested by the Arms of Galway, shows a golden ship, and on the rigging an escutcheon in black enamel, charged with a golden lion rampant. Beneath the ship are the waves of the sea and the words GALWAY 1908, and around above the ship, incised in the bronze, the words TRADE BEYOND THE SEAS.

would have subscribed himself with this *Mise*, meaning 'I am Aodh Ó Néill (or whoever he was) and let none dare to say otherwise'. There must have been few fathers who in like circumstances and with his upbringing would have replied thus and with such care not to pour scorn on this new practice in official letter writing.

In the course of time, my father came to realize that he was dissipating his energies to such an extent, that he was not doing any serious academic writing. His professor at Trinity College Dublin, the Shakespearean scholar, Edward Dowden, was still in the chair of English Literature in Dublin having occupied it since it was founded in 1867, four years after Dowden had graduated. This tenure of office had to come to an end sometime, and my father set his heart on at least being in the running for that chair, when it should become vacant. He therefore decided to concentrate on what was to be his major work, *Shakespeare's Hamlet: A New Commentary, with a chapter on First Principles.* To this end he gave up his chair in Galway and retired to the country to write his book.

He had married in 1903, at the age of thirty, Mary Alicia Cross, who was of a County Cork farming family. She was never very strong, and in Galway she suffered much from asthma, a much more troublesome complaint then than now. Medical advice was that she should live at a certain height above sea level, and remain at that height. The village of Blessington, County Wicklow, seemed to combine this possibility with the advantage of relative proximity to Dublin, so the family moved there in 1912.

My father resigned his chair in Galway in December 1912. Dowden died in April 1913. My father's work on *Hamlet* was not completed, but he now rushed it through and got it published in June 1913. This enabled him to make a serious application for the chair of English Literature in Dublin University (TCD). He was appointed to the chair in November 1913 and held it until his death in 1939.

For the first few years in his new appointment, he used to drive the nineteen miles from Blessington to Dublin at a spanking pace in the spider, a very light one-horse carriage with a high body and large slender wheels. He would stable the horse at Sewell's

The Blessington steam-tram

stables, at the corner of Merrion Square East and Lower Mount Street, and spend a few nights in his rooms at 39 TCD before driving back to Blessington at a much slower pace up the long hill from Tallaght to Crooksling and Brittas. The spider was a two-seater, but we children would sometimes sit on the floor at the back, with our legs dangling out at the rear.

Our house, Downshire Lodge, was one of the two largest houses in Blessington. It occupied one side of the village square and is now the Ulster Bank. There was a steam-tram which ran along the road, a regular service between Terenure and Blessington, and on to Pollaphuca Waterfall in the summer. It was fun for us children on the rare occasions when we travelled on it, but terrifying for the high-spirited horse to see it approach.

One of my earliest recollections is of seeing the village square full of British soldiers and horse-drawn artillery. This was during Easter week 1916. The Rural District Council of Blessington passed a resolution welcoming the soldiers who had come to protect the village from unknown terrors. My father used to say that when the executions of the 1916 leaders began, the members of the RDC were so ashamed at their having welcomed the troops, that they literally rescinded the minute by actually cutting it out of the Minute Book. I have searched but have been unable to find the Minute Book or any record of these proceedings.

The senior officers were billeted on us as long as they remained in Blessington. When they left, my father found that he was missing a carriage clock, which they had evidently taken as a souvenir. Otherwise they did us no harm.

An earlier recollection, is that of the visit of one of our first cousins, of whom we only ever possessed four. Fergus Chalmers Wright came to stay with us soon after the outbreak of war in 1914. He was a refugee from Belgium, where his family had been living for some years, and where he was brought up with French as his first language and the language which he always spoke with his twin sister, Dreda.

Our first cousins were all on our mother's side. The absence of such cousins on Father's side arose from the fact that he was an only son and that his three sisters never married. Their mother was Janetta Wilbraham Taylor, daughter of Wilbraham Taylor, of Hadley Hurst, Barnet, in Hertfordshire. Taylor was Gentleman Usher to Queen Victoria and Secretary to the Privy Purse. Hadley Hurst was a Georgian mansion full of beautiful things in which, in his youth, my father delighted. They were for him, he said, his 'links with the cultural history of the ages'. All was dispersed upon the death of Wilbraham Taylor in 1875. I presume that it was in order for the holder of that office to keep the oak chest bearing the brass plate engraved 'Secretary Privy Purse'; the chest is now in my possession.

We were in the process of moving from Blessington to Dublin coming up to Easter 1916 and were back in Blessington for the Easter break. In Dublin we had had temporary accommodation in 9 Herbert Street, which I remember as being very tall and narrow with very steep stairs, quite unlike Downshire Lodge. I remember the excitement of travelling, for whatever reason, in the dark, along lamp-lit streets on the top of an open-topped tram.

An open-top tram of the Dublin United Tramways Company, destination Clontarf
Photo: W.A. Camwell

Our first home in Dublin was at 6 Clyde Road, directly opposite Saint Bartholomew's Church. This church was too 'high' for my parents and we used to go to Saint Mary's Church, Donnybrook, on the corner of Simmonscourt Road.

We had the pony and traps in the stables at the bottom of the garden, with access to Clyde Lane. We must have been back there very soon after the Easter Rising, and while life in the city and suburbs was still unsettled. There were no deliveries to the house and I remember being in the pony trap, the tub, and being stopped and searched by British military on our way to get bread from Johnston Mooney & O'Brien's bakery at Ball's Bridge and other supplies.

I remember little of the impact of the Great War except that we ate margarine, while butter had to be supplied to the kitchen staff, including two girls called Hickey, from County Kerry, who were ardent supporters of Sinn Féin and, later, of Éamon de Valera. Unlike all our neighbours, we had no members of the family or near relatives, or indeed anyone that we children knew, in the British forces. This arose partly from the fact that we had so few near relatives. My mother had three younger sisters, two of whom were married and had children; but they all lived in England and we had almost no contact with them.

When the war came to an end, every house in Clyde Road hung out a Union Jack. But not No. 6. My parents had been preparing a different sort of flag, the flag not of victory, but of peace, and I remember seeing them working at it — a white sheet with a large blue dove on it. They had none of the generally accepted attitudes towards the war and the Germans. My father, for one thing, was greatly concerned about the fate of his father's sister, Helen, his beloved 'Aunt Zinnie', who in 1874 had married Moritz von Bernus of Frankfurt-am-Main and was living there, throughout the war.

In Blessington we had a governess, though I do not remember her; and she must have taught us some French, as well as piano lessons, for I remember the sentence *où est mon chat?* from which I never forgot that *où* meaning 'where' had an accent on it.

In Clyde Road, the three of us younger children went to a school at the end of the road, run by the Misses Wilson, Florence and Edith. Up to 1914 it had been the German High School; probably the Misses Wilson had trained or taught in Germany. With the outbreak of war it became the High School (not to be confused with a boys' school of the same name), and in our day it was called Nightingale Hall, a clear association of Florence Wilson with Florence Nightingale. It had a kindergarten (note the German influence) and in the lower classes of the school itself, there were boys and girls together; but by the time I was eight or nine years old, I was the only boy in my class, which I did not like at all, and the girls would tease me sometimes about the peculiar clothes I wore — cast-offs from my cousin, Edo Wright. So I was glad to be sent to a boarding school for boys, Baymount Preparatory School, Dollymount, Dublin — preparatory, that is, 'for the English public schools and the Royal Navy'.

II

Preparatory School

It was at Baymount that I first became aware of being an Irish nationalist and of being different in this respect from, as far as I know, all my school-fellows. The Anglo-Irish War was then at its height. Michael Collins became my hero and I pasted newspaper cuttings of him to the inside of my locker door.

I had some knowledge of nationalist songs such as 'A Nation Once Again'. On Sundays we used to go for walks in 'crocodile' formation to the Bull Wall, leading to the North Bull, a large sandbank island in Dublin Bay. Returning in crocodile formation from one of these walks, as we entered the school grounds, I thought to enliven the proceedings by singing the song of 'Clare's Dragoons'. It is a good marching song, but nobody sang with me. Its recollection of Irish military success against the Saxon foe may have made it unacceptable in the British homes to which all those boys belonged, even though it referred to something as remote as the War of the Spanish Succession in the Netherlands. The master in charge of that walk did not know the song, and went to take a swipe at me when he heard the word 'bloody', before he realized that I really meant bloody. I must have learnt words and music from Paddy and have never forgotten them. The opening lines are: 'When on Ramillies bloody field/ The baffled French were forced to yield,/ The victor Saxon backward reeled/Before the charge of Clare's dragoons./ The flags we conquered in that fray/ Look lone on Ypres tower, they say,/ So we'll win them company to-day/ Or bravely die like Clare's dragoons'.

I was tremendously elated by the news that the Irish Free State had been established The news was given to us in class with a clear signal that the Free State was now to command our loyalty. There was one boy, Peter Thornhill, who struck me as being least likely to feel such loyalty. I amused myself by painting the Irish tricolour on a sheet of paper and putting it in front of him. He immediately tore it up, which delighted me, because at the same time he tore up the Union Jack which I had drawn on the other side.

I do not know how I came by my nationalist feelings. I do not recollect ever having heard politics discussed at home, and I was away from home when our house at 26 Clyde Road (to which we had moved from no. 6) was raided by British military. The reason for the raid was apparently that Father was found to be on a list of subscribers to *The Bulletin*. This was a cyclostyled news-sheet, issued by the Sinn Féin Department of Publicity from November 1919, and appearing several times a week. Its value was its day-to-day factual account of what was going on, including British acts of aggression, and it was an antidote to the false propaganda from the British side. It was largely written by Erskine Childers, the first of that name, and was of course regarded as highly seditious. The Department of Publicity was in the charge of Desmond FitzGerald who, his son Garret later told me, had had the experience of running an undergraduate newspaper for five years, in which he published nothing unless he was certain that it was true.

My parents were actively involved in the Parents' National Educational Union, and Father was for a time President of the Dublin branch. The PNEU was primarily intended to help parents who were teaching their children at home. In this connection 'Musical Evenings' were held in various private houses, and perhaps once a year they would be in our house. Various children would come and perform the works of one particular composer whom they had all been studying. My sister-in-law, Cerise (Orpen) Parker, shortly before her death in 1990, recalled such an evening conducted by my father on these lines – Father: 'Chopin was born in Warsaw of poor but worthy parents. My son, Patrick, who is at

St Columba's College and has been let out for the day, will now play (such and such a piece) on the flute'. Paddy plays and Father says another sentence or two about Chopin, and then – 'Grace Orpen will now play (such and such) on the piano'. At tea, the lights fail and one of the maids comes in and says, 'Master Chal (that's me!), will you please turn on the lights'. The lights, by the way, were gas, not electricity.

I have no recollection of that incident; but Cerise cannot have invented that bit about Master Chal. Her younger sister, Bea, who was later to become my wife, had a somewhat different recollection of the same occasion. She said they hated those evenings, and having to play very likely the same piece as several other children had played. There was, after all, a limit to the number of pieces that children could play by the one composer. She remembered that at tea-time the main decoration on the wall was a map of the drainage system of the house. That is what hung on the wall of the ante-room to Father's study at Woodview, on the Stillorgan Road, where we lived for a few years in the 1920s. Bea recalled Father saying, 'Mrs Trench is upstairs in bed, children, and I want you to play loudly so that she can hear'. I can only say that I hope that she was not right about that, and that Father was not that insensitive about music.

Paddy was quite musical, as we all were. He was the most versatile, playing flute, piccolo, tin-whistle and the American organ. This last was an unusual instrument; in fact I don't think I ever saw another one. Otherwise called a cabinet organ, it was like a very superior harmonium; but instead of the air being blown through reeds, as in the harmonium, it was sucked through them and produced a tone like a pipe organ. It had two manuals, and may have had pedals. We had it a short time at Woodview, and only a short time — I don't know why. It was put into McCullough's at 56 Dawson Street, to be sold, and it and the whole premises were completely destroyed by a mine explosion on 29 December 1922. The premises belonged to Denis McCullough. He had been in Dawson Street for about twelve months, having been burnt out of Belfast by Orangemen. He had been working for twenty years in the Republican cause, he said; but he supported the Free State, so he had to be burnt out again. He rebuilt his musical instruments business and his family were the owners and directors of the McCullough Pigott concern until they sold their interest in 1993.

In May 1921, the Musical Evening was at 26 Clyde Road, and I was allowed home for it. On the way back, from the top of the tram along Clontarf Road, I saw the Custom House ablaze, set on fire and totally destroyed by Republican forces. There was a parents' cricket match at Baymount that day, and it was said that one of the fathers stooped to pick up a charred piece of paper which had landed at his feet, and that he identified it as coming from his own office in the Custom House.

I think that the teaching at Baymount must have been quite good, although, typically of those preparatory schools, there was a fairly frequent turn-over of 'unqualified' male teachers, all I suppose recently demobilized from the British forces after the World War. One was evidently suffering from shell-shock and an unexpected noise in the class-room had the most terrifying effect on him. An unfortunate boy called Greer accidentally let his pencil case or something fall from his desk and that master produced a cane (which was forbidden); it was the only time I ever saw a boy being savagely beaten, on the hands. I reported the matter to the teacher whom I liked best, Miss Magowan, and that master did not come back after that term. The only graduate, apart from the headmaster, William Lucas Scott, was Miss Magowan, who taught French and German, and perhaps English Literature too, for I think that she had something to do with the extracts from *As You Like It* which we performed. I had the part of Jacques, and can still recite the speeches I learnt then, though I remember nothing of what I learnt by heart at a later date.

I had quite a good boy's singing voice and I liked singing in the choir of the church we attended. That was the parish church of Raheny, set in the grounds of Saint Anne's, now a beautiful public park, but then the residence of Lady Ardilaun, widow of one of the many Arthur Guinnesses. I enjoyed the walk through these spacious grounds and particularly my right as a chorister to ride my bike through them in the summer term. Once I actually penetrated the marble halls of Saint Anne's (of which not a trace remains) taken there by my father to have afternoon tea with Lady Ardilaun in splendid solitude.

I was not unhappy at Baymount and was quite glad to be sent on to another boarding school, which in any case was normal practice at my parents' social level. Home had its limitations. Father was fairly remote and Mother was an invalid, at least from the time we left Galway, suffering from asthma, arthritis and, later, very painful eye trouble. In Clyde Road she would sometimes go out in the pony-trap, or tub, which any of us could drive. We also had a horse-drawn Bath chair for her — most unusual, if not unique, in Ireland. I remember driving it, wearing my Baymount cap, blazer and socks, seated on the apron of the chair, arousing derision from passing boys who would sometimes give a whack to the pony, if they had a stick handy.

If our parents had any shortcomings as parents, this may be blamed on the tragedy and frustration which marked their married life. They had four children in the first six years of their marriage. Thereafter Mother's illness must have meant an early end to their intimate relationship. She was never strong, though she recalled that once in Galway, when she had left Paddy as a baby in the pony-trap with the nurse for a moment, and the pony bolted off without her, she ran and caught up with it with a vigour and strength which she knew she did not possess on her own.

She suffered greatly from asthma, relieved only by the inhalation of drugs such as amyl nitrate, which in the long run no doubt affected her heart. Worse still was the rheumatoid arthritis which crippled and distorted her hands and eventually affected her whole body, including her eyes, which caused her great pain. For the last years of her life she sat in a corner of the drawing-room of Grianblah, with blinds drawn; Grianblah was the house which Father built in 1928 in the grounds of Balnagowan, Palmerston Park. She would start with pain if anyone entered the room and caused a flash of light to reach her. She had the wireless beside her, her life-line, and listened to everything, mostly on 2LO (London), except football and

Woodview, Stillorgan Road, Dublin, the Trench family home, 1921-25.
Now part of the Faculty of Medicine, UCD, Belfield

The author in Baymount Prep. School blazer, driving his mother in the Bath chair,
with Sheela and Shamrock walking alongside, c. 1920

jazz, as she said. Father must have spent a fortune on medical care for her over some twenty years. My sister Sheela's recollection is that they were very badly advised and that whenever Mother seemed to be benefitting from the treatment prescribed by the doctor, who came from Dundrum to attend her for many years, he changed the treatment and she got worse again.

I do not remember any holidays with our parents but I believe that we did visit our grandparents in our early childhood several times. Both sets of grandparents had gone to live in England. For the sea crossing we would each be given Mothersill tablets to prevent sea-sickness, the tablet being hidden in a strawberry. There is a photo of us as quite small children on a switch-back at Winscales, near Workington, where my father's parents lived. (This is not to be confused with the Windscale which became known, or notorious, as Sellafield. Winscales in fact became a training centre for rescue workers in the mines). We knew the three Winscales aunts quite well. They had Pekingese dogs who were of a sporting nature and would go out with the cat to catch rabbits. There were hedgehogs who came to the door regularly for their saucer of milk, and there were moles who raised lumps in the croquet lawn. We had rides on the horse and we watched Aunt Gertrude separating cream in the dairy. She also drove the Model T Ford.

We did not like Granny Trench and her questioning of us had we been 'saved', that is to say, converted to the view of God and Jesus Christ held by the Plymouth Brethren. She was the one who decided that none of the men who courted her daughters — at least two of whom were very handsome — were good enough for them. So they remained unmarried, and devoted their lives to work for the blind.

At Hollywood, in Somerset, on the other hand, Granny Cross, Mother's stepmother, is remembered as a very sweet little doll-like figure with ringlets. And Aunt Edel, the only one of Mother's sisters to remain at home and unmarried, would lift us up on to the great hunter. She supplied the girls with breeches, which seemed remarkable in one whose own dress was so extremely old-fashioned. I visited there with Father, when I was thirteen years old,

Three generations: the author and his brother Patrick, with their father and grandfather, at Winscales, Aug. 1920

on my way to Repton School for the first time. I was wearing an Eton jacket, the bum-freezer as it was called, and I wore that for only my first term, since I soon discovered that the morning coat was the correct wear for a boy of my size. I went to the Brethren's meeting at Portishead, and was asked by complete strangers whether I had been saved. I certainly replied yes, even if I did not understand what the question meant. I was not going to risk any other answer.

Apart from these visits to grandparents, I remember no holidays, except once at Malahide with Father's second cousin, May Kemmis, who beat her daughter with a riding crop, and once at Lisheen, Sligo, the home of Basil Phibbs and his wife, née Taylor, their sons Denis and Geoffrey (who changed his name to Taylor, because he so disliked his father), and daughter Maeve. And once I had a summer holiday at Galway Grammar School where I am pretty sure that the headmaster, Eraut, also had a family connection with us. His son was at Baymount with me. That is all I can remember of childhood holidays. I never knew what family holidays could be like, until I met and married Bea Orpen and learnt of the Orpen family gatherings in Donegal for twenty-seven consecutive years.

As for our parents, they did some touring in Conamara in the spider; but apart from that they got away together for only two journeys that I know of. Both were to the south of France. From Biarritz Mother carried home two green water-jugs which I still possess. At Easter time 1914 they were in Vernet-les-Bains, Carcassonne and Paris.

Father had a passionate nature and a quick temper, which he struggled, manfully, to control. Sheela was terrified of him. I do not remember being so, but Sheela was much closer to him and for many more years than I. One of her alarming experiences had to do with Paddy's republican activities. He entered TCD in October 1922, just three days before the Bill approving the constitution of the Irish Free State was passed in the Dáil, when the country was split between Free Staters and Republicans. The Anglo-Irish War had come to an end with the truce of 11 July 1921, followed by the Treaty of December 1921; but civil war broke out between the pro-

Treaty and anti-Treaty factions and continued until 24 May 1923. Paddy sided with the Republicans, that is to say, against the Treaty. He, along with other students, had some clashes with the Dublin Metropolitan Police and a police helmet was captured and was on display in his rooms in college. He also had a knuckle-duster, the only one I ever saw.

Paddy confided to Sheela in great secrecy that he was to carry despatches on his motor-bike from Dublin to the Republican forces in the south, passing through the main area of hostilities between the opposing forces. When it was reported that he had disappeared, Sheela was torn with doubt as to whether she should tell her parents about the despatch riding. They were frantically distracted at his disappearance in those troubled times and she decided to tell them. They were then even more distracted as to what might happen to him on his dangerous journey through the front line of hostilities. He came back safely and told Sheela that of course he intended that she should tell the parents what she knew once he was well on his way.

Paddy's fellow Republicans in TCD included Alec Newman and R.M.Hilliard, now both dead. I think it was Newman who was Paddy's pillion passenger on his escapade down south. Newman graduated (which Paddy never did) in 1926, joined *The Irish Times* as a journalist in 1930 and was editor from 1954 until he resigned in 1961. He died in 1972.

Bob Hilliard was a Kerryman, a keen athlete and a boxer of Olympics standard, holding the Irish featherweight title for two years.While at TCD he became actively involved in the civil war, on the anti-Treaty side. He left TCD without a degree and went to London where I remember him about 1929 as a tough, hard-drinking, hard-swearing Fleet Street journalist. He came under the influence of the Moral Rearmament movement, returned to Dublin, took his degree, was ordained in the Church of Ireland and worked with the Belfast Cathedral mission in some of the toughest areas of Belfast. He continued to box, which no doubt endeared him to his large working-class congregations. He had married an Englishwoman but things went badly wrong. He went to London and joined the International Brigade in Spain. Wounded at the Battle of Jarama, he was taken to hospital and died there when the hospital was bombed in February 1937. The death of *el pastor protestante, Reverendo Hilliard* is one of those singled out in the history of the battle *(Guerra y Revolucion in España, 1936-39,* Moscu, 1966, II, 247). Wherever the Irishmen who fought and died in the Spanish war on the Republican side are commemorated, he is remembered as the Protestant clergyman who was one of them.

I have strayed from what was to have been the main subject of this chapter, namely Baymount Preparatory School. Baymount is now called Manresa House and is a Jesuit retreat centre, with an oratory specially constructed to contain five splendid stained glass windows by Evie Hone, formerly in the Jesuit chapel at Tullabeg, County Offaly.

III

Repton

At the age of 13, after four years as a boarder at Baymount Preparatory School, I was sent to school in England. I had sat for entrance scholarship into Repton and though I was not successful I did get my place. It was a long-established tradition for many generations, for Irish families of a certain social and financial standing to send their sons to school in England. This applied to both Catholic and Protestant families. Furthermore, it was 1923, when Ireland was just recovering from the Anglo-Irish War and the subsequent civil war. Education, like everything, was in a parlous state and it was natural for my parents to consider that England offered a better all-round education than was obtainable in Ireland.

I was bad at making friends, then as later, and I never again wished to see the boys who were at Baymount. So I was very glad to be sent to a school in England where I was unlikely to meet them. They mostly went to Shrewsbury, or to St Columba's College, Rathfarnham, County Dublin. I do not know why my parents chose Repton, nor indeed what they knew about public schools at all; but it was a good choice. It was one of the old public schools, founded in 1557 and incorporating much of a 12th-century Augustinian priory, set in the village of Repton in Derbyshire, once the capital of the Anglo-Saxon kingdom of Mercia. It had about 400 boys (but we all called ourselves men), divided into eight houses. These were actual houses scattered round the village, each housing about forty boys, except the Hall, which had something over eighty boys, and that is where I was, again a good choice as far as I was concerned. This was the house of the headmaster, Geoffrey Fisher. He had been appointed Head of Repton in 1914 at the exceptionally young age of twenty-seven.

There was keen rivalry between the houses in all games and keen loyalty to one's own house. One hardly knew, and certainly did not mix with, anyone in a house other than one's own. Because of its size, the Hall was divided into two halves for competitive purposes, A-K and L-Z. So at inter-house football matches I shouted 'L-TO-Z'. After my first year I was not interested in shouting at sports at all.

I was never in any of the other houses and had no idea what life was like there; but in the Hall, the oldest of the houses, we lived in studies of five or six boys, namely, the study-holder in his fourth or fifth year, one or two 'seconds' in their third or fourth year, and two 'fags' in their first or second year. Fagging has received much adverse comment, associating it with bullying and beating. It was not like that in my experience. Fags were required to keep the tiny study clean and tidy, and they may have been expected to clean the study-holder's boots and shoes and to run messages for him. A few of the senior study-holders were also prefects. A prefect was entitled to stand at the door of his study and roar 'F-a-a-g' down the corridor. Then we all had to drop whatever we were doing and run to see what he wanted. I remember this happening only once.

In theory, the study-holder had the right to beat his fags for any misdemeanour, and the prefects had the right to beat anyone, but I never knew it to happen, except that I was once beaten by the head of the house, three years my senior, for something I had not done, namely 'fooling around on the football field'. It was just that my foot movements were uncoordinated, and I had no idea that anyone had thought I was fooling. Nothing was said to me at the time; but when I was faced with the accusation, I was too frightened to deny it. I wanted to get the whole ordeal over. Six strokes of the cane on the bottom, dressed only in pyjamas, I found a very painful and humiliating experience which I certainly was not going to inflict on anyone else. Nor did any of my generation. And there was no bullying that I knew of. I was lucky in this respect. Earlier and later generations, I learned, did indulge in beatings.

Charles Smyth was at the Hall from 1916 and left just two years before I arrived. He became a professional historian, as well as a Canon of Westminster. He recalls that for almost half of his time at Repton the school lived under the threatening shadow of the war. He considers that it was an indirect consequence of this that there were probably more beatings than there would have been under normal conditions, although most of his generation of fags in the Hall, himself included, he says, were fortunate in this particular respect.

John Orpen went to Repton one year before me and was at Latham House. His father was a fourth cousin of Bea's; but he lived in England all his life and I did not meet him, nor indeed know of him, until after her death. Latham had the same study system as the Hall. John confirms that beating was not prevalent in his day. Like myself, he was beaten only once.

I could have been a prime target for hostility because I was Irish. Practically every other boy there must have lost a near relative in the war which had ended just five years before I entered Repton. Conscription was introduced in England for the first time in January 1916 and five months later was extended to cover all men between the ages of eighteen and forty-one. This meant that every boy at Repton and elsewhere was called up on precisely his eighteenth birthday, regardless of whether he was in the middle of his final exams. If, having spent four years or so in the Officers' Training Corps, or 'the Corps' as it was called at Repton, he had Certificate A, his call-up was delayed to age eighteen-and-a-half and he was given a commission. His life expectancy from that date was three weeks, Charles Smyth says. Ponder that obscenity for a moment.

So my contemporaries at Repton would have lost their elder brothers, fathers, uncles, cousins or other relatives and would also have heard it said that the Irish stabbed England in the back in 1916; but I never heard a word of this from them. My housemaster (he was an army captain and became a major while I was there) called me affectionately 'the mad Irishman' and others called me 'Sinn Féiner' as a term of abuse. I laughed to myself because I really was a Sinn Féiner.

Words like milk and film, which I pronounced as almost two syllables were grounds for some mockery. Even the Head thought it hilarious. Squirrel was another problem. In French class, no doubt my first term, the master asked, 'Anyone know what *écureuil* means?' 'Squirrel', I replied promptly. The class burst into laughter. 'Yes, that's right', said the master, 'squrrel' — pronouncing the u as in put, whereas I pronounced that first syllable with a short i as in squid.

I don't think I ever changed my pronunciation, but in other respects I was determined to conform and to be as inconspicuous as possible. I was terrified to begin with, after all I had heard about public schools. Conformity included joining the corps. Father had found out that it was voluntary and would have preferred me not to join; but I discovered that everyone who was not physically incapable was in it, and I wasn't going to stay out, much as I disliked it. I soon got into the drums and bugles band. I played the bugle and enjoyed that. Of course I had to do a certain amount of square-bashing, rifle drill and button-polishing and getting used to that extraordinary article of dress, the puttee, adopted from India as part of the uniform of the British soldier.

We had shooting practice too, with ·22 ammunition; but I was found to be a hopeless, and unenthusiastic, marksman and I volunteered for target duty with teams who went to some more distant rifle range where service rifles and ammunition were used. My job was in the pit behind the targets, but what exactly I did I don't remember. It was infra dig, but it was a change from routine; it meant an excursion into the country and was better than playing football or cricket, at both of which I was useless. I much preferred cross-country running, which I was often detailed to do by myself or with others who were not good enough to play on the first three house teams.

Once a year the corps would go on a Field Day. We would go by train for an hour or two and divide into two armies for a mock battle. The best of it was when I was chosen to be signaller, and while the others were tramping across the countryside, or crawling on their bellies with their heavy packs and rifles, I would stand with the staff officers carrying nothing but a bugle, with which I was supposed to be able to give signals to the troops; but I had never been told how this was to be done.

Then there was the annual summer camp, at one of the regular army bases, under canvas. This was the cause of much grumbling, but I was determined to get some fun out of it. My turn came in 1925, at the end of my second year, and I was bold enough to be able to declare that I was going to camp, that I was going to enjoy it, and that I was then going to leave the corps. Nobody believed me. Nobody ever left the corps; or so it was thought.

At camp I volunteered for fatigue duty which meant that while, again, the others were sweating about in their bull's wool uniforms, I stayed in camp, wore dungarees, helped the kitchen staff, fed the troops, washed up, and actually enjoyed the experience of being under canvas for a week.

To get home on the free rail pass, one had to be in uniform, up to and including the mail boat from Holyhead. I warned Father of this and he met me at Dún Laoghaire with an overcoat to hide my khaki uniform. I then got him to write to the Head under the heading 'Disarmament or Armageddon', to say that he and I wished me to resign from the corps and not to attend any more parades. Fisher acknowledged Father's letter; he did not agree with it, but he respected our wishes.

The accepted thing to do after attending camp was to sit for the Certificate A exam. Passing this exam put one on the officer reserve, with the guarantee of a commission in the event of a call-up. When I returned to Repton for the next term, I saw my name posted for parade as usual. I did not attend and that was the end of that.

It could be very cold in Derbyshire, colder than anything I had known in Ireland. Nevertheless, first thing every morning, summer and winter, we ran naked down the corridors and plunged into a cold bath. The coldest experience was standing on the touch-line during school football matches to cheer on the team. Repton was one of the few front-line public schools to play soccer rather than rugby. Fisher maintained the soccer tradition because it was the game of 'the people' in England, though in fact rugby was the people's game in Wales. Fisher was concerned that public school men should mix with the sons of miners and other workers. Reptonians and Old Reptonians in London took part in the running of the Repton Club in Bethnal Green, which had been started there in 1894, 'providing for the improvement of health, education and recreation, and to develop a community spirit' in that poor neighbourhood in the East End of London.

There was no question of my taking part in any such activity in London; but I was interested to hear social and economic problems discussed, and for this I joined the Civics Class, a voluntary extra for senior forms. It had been started by Victor Gollancz, who was on the staff at Repton for some eighteen months during the war, having been given a commission but declared unfit for active service because of deficient eyesight. In his autobiographical writings, the *Timothy* books, he has given a critical account of Repton, for which, however, he shows a clear affection. Charles Smyth described his account as being spattered with slovenly inaccuracies.

Roald Dahl's *Boy: Tales of Childhood* (London, 1984) is another book which gives a very different picture from mine of life at Repton and of its headmaster, Geoffrey Fisher. Dahl was born in 1916 and entered Repton in 1930, three years after I had left. His generation, seems to have indulged to some extent in the appalling practice of senior boys caning other boys for trivial misdemeanours, which my generation in the Hall did not do. Dahl describes a particularly sadistic caning by Fisher, but this was not an experience he had had himself. No doubt the incident, if it ever happened, was well embellished in the telling to him and greatly more so by him, prince of story-tellers.

I got pleurisy during my second term at Repton and was seriously ill in the school sanatorium. There was some question of Father being summoned to my bedside, but I rallied before this was considered necessary. My parents decided that what I needed was a warm overcoat, and they got a special one 'built' for me. I say built because it was of enormous proportions. It was beautifully made, black, with a lamb's wool lining. It was much longer than was normal and it had a very large collar. It was so unlike anything any other boy had that I certainly wasn't going to take it back to school with me. I came to love it in later years and was still wearing it forty-five years later.

There was a fair amount of musical activity at Repton for those who wanted it. I had piano lessons with Miss Penny Forman. She lived in the Hall with the Head and Mrs Fisher. She was one of Mrs Fisher's eleven siblings. As a teacher, she was not very demanding and did not require hours of scales and arpeggios. I enjoyed my lessons, and my practice in the sound-proofed cubicles of the Music Schools. I played at the School Concert after Speech Day in June 1927. That is to say, I and another boy pianist together accompanied six boys singing *Liebeslieder Waltz No. 6* by Brahms. My father was there for that weekend, the only time he came to Repton after leaving me there in 1923. I had asked him to come, as this would be the last opportunity before my final year; but I don't think he enjoyed it and I found him rather an embarrassment.

I sang with the Repton School Musical Society. The most ambitious work I remember doing there had a distinctly Irish flavour. It was Sir Charles Villiers Stanford's *Phaudrig Crohoore.* I also sang German lieder and in the chapel choir, which made chapel attendance more enjoyable. There were many occasions when the national anthem was sung. I never acknowledged the king as our king, but I found it was possible to sing 'God save *your* gracious king' without anyone noticing, and this salved my conscience. When we sang Blake's *Jerusalem* to Parry's music, which was in the Repton School Hymn Book, I was similarly able to question whether those feet in ancient time did 'Walk upon Ireland's mountains green', whether the Lamb of God was 'On Ireland's pleasant pastures seen' and whether we should not build the new Jerusalem 'In Ireland's green and pleasant land'.

I occasionally visited the homes of two of my modern

languages masters for, in one case, a gramophone recital, and in the other, chamber music played by the master and his family. There were occasional concerts for the whole school, with visiting performers, of whom I remember particularly Myra Hess (piano) and Jelly d'Aranyi (violin) playing together.

On one occasion Fisher took me, with one other boy, to Derby, eight miles from Repton, for a performance of Elgar's oratorio, *The Dream of Gerontius,* a dramatic poem by Cardinal Newman. I had never been to a public performance of any kind, except a Shakespeare performance in the Iveagh Gardens in Dublin, and I was enormously impressed. It was a privilege to be selected by the Head for this experience. I greatly enjoyed Sunday evenings, sitting on the floor of the Head's drawing-room, singing madrigals with him and Mrs Fisher and a chosen few.

I became very enthusiastic about Beethoven and had the names of 'Ludwig' or 'Beethoven' attached to me, partly because of my unruly hair. When I left, I presented a portrait of Beethoven to hang in the classroom where I had learnt German. There was, I might add, a mighty gulf between those of us who were interested in serious or classical music and those who played the mandolin and the banjo, as many did.

In 1925, at age fifteen-and-a-half, which was about normal, I passed the School Certificate exam (set by the Oxford and Cambridge Schools Examination Board) with distinctions in English, Maths, French, German and Latin. Thereafter I specialized in my chosen subjects — the language and literature, history, art history, and philosophy of France and Germany, and nothing else. No maths, the only subject I ever got a prize in, no science, no Latin.

I certainly enjoyed my last two years, studying the things that interested me and reaching a higher standard in languages than I could have done in a less specialized system, such as obtained in Ireland; but I came to doubt the wisdom of specialization at so early an age, particularly when I sat before interview boards and discovered my abysmal lack of general knowledge. John Orpen had a similar experience. He studied classics at Repton and history at Cambridge. He then joined a firm of solicitors in Brighton and has remained there for the rest of his life. He was astonished at the general knowledge of the clerks, who had no public school and university education, and found himself to be ignorant of science, as well as being bad at maths.

Another way in which the curriculum at Repton differed from that in Irish schools was a reduced concentration on set books. We were given long reading lists and were encouraged to read widely outside them. I cannot now recall any details, except my surprise at being recommended in history class to read *Napoleon,* a poetic play by Herbert Trench, who was a first cousin of my father's. There was a very good library, which I loved, particularly when I had freed myself from OTC parades. I remember writing to my father and telling him of my delight at 'discovering' Shakespeare's Sonnets, which nobody had told me about.

Sonnet CXVI ('Let me not to the marriage of true minds/ Admit impediments') is one of the few things I remember learning by heart of my own volition, and when I was in Cambridge I cut a one-off disc of myself reciting it. That was a thing one could easily do for a small charge and it made a nice present for someone whose native language was not English and who said that she liked the way I pronounced the word 'love'.

Here is an affectionate picture of the school library, which I can endorse, except that I am not familiar with the Bodleian. It is by Richard Coe, who was at Repton from 1937 to 1941, and it appeared in the Repton School Terminal Letter, May 1991, as an extract from his autobiography, which was privately published by his widow in 1992.

> The Library at Repton is its greatest glory. It is a Bodleian in miniature; indeed, among the great libraries of the world, only the Bodleian has ever given me a similar sensation. Housed in a lofty chamber, remnant of the ancient monastic foundation out of which the school was destined eventually to grow, its walls are fashioned of rough grey stone softened with panelling, and its ceiling is of carved black-and-gilt beams. The sunlight intrudes through the tall, mullioned windows, lying in soft, golden pools on the polished tables; and the high shelving

> is clamorous with the sheer beauty of books. It is an Aladdin's Cave; and this, now that I am given the sudden freedom of it, is my first and most enduring impression: the shock of something indescribably beautiful. It is like plunging my arms up to the elbows in a casket of jewellery — and then each jewel opens up, to reveal further, even more miraculous jewels inside.

There were very few Irish boys at Repton, and none ever travelled with me in either direction. In July 1927 I was greatly distressed to hear of the assassination of Kevin O'Higgins, Minister for Justice and External Affairs, and felt that I must share my grief with someone, so I said to the one other boy in the Hall who was from Ireland, 'Did you hear that Kevin O'Higgins has been assassinated?' He laughed and said, 'And who might he be?' I never exchanged another word with him about Ireland.

In the summer of 1926 I went to the south of France for a vacation course. The franc was at such a low value that it was cheaper to go to the south of France than to come home. The course was run by the University of Toulouse at Bagnères-de-Bigorre, a beautifully situated spa in the Hautes Pyrénées. I was by now becoming an experienced traveller, having done sixteen journeys between Dublin and Repton by myself.

The journey to the south of France included a day or two in Paris and then a fourteen-hour train journey, all on my own. We were housed in a lycée, in dormitories, each of us occupying a cubicle, in which the only light was a candle.

The course was not brilliant, but the vacation was. At the end of it, the University of Toulouse awarded me a Certificat d'Etudes Françaises, which was valueless. What was important for me was that for the first time I had seen mountains capped by eternal snows and had climbed up into them.

I went into the Pyrenees with two young men, a Belgian and a Scot, and two Norwegian girls. Coach tours were so cheap that we did not mind paying for a round trip and leaving it at the halfway mark, the mountain resort of Gavarnie. From there we climbed for about six hours, passing from the scorching heat of an extra hot first day of September to the freezing cold of a snow-covered col at about 9,000 feet above sea level, or 4,000 feet above Gavarnie. We spent the night in a hut on a bed of straw spread across a raised platform. We shared the bed with some French and English mountaineers, complete with ropes and ice-axes, who were going to ascend the Mont Perdu (19,944 feet). I had acquired a pair of boots, iron shod *pour la haute montagne,* but none of our party was equipped for the extreme cold of the night, except for some bottles of Bénédictine. We were up early and at least put our feet into Spain, but we came down on the French side again. The whole experience thrilled me.

Another thrilling excursion was to the Pic du Midi de Bigorre (9,439 feet) to see the sunrise in the mountains. And I went on my own to Lourdes, by the electric tram which ran along the road from Bagnères, a distance of 22 km.

In the next school year, 1926–27, I sat for an entrance scholarship to Cambridge. I was unsuccessful as far as the scholarship was concerned, but I won my place. I had selected Sidney Sussex College as one which offered Modern Languages scholarships without too much emphasis on Latin; but I did have to polish up some Latin in order to do the Latin translation papers for Modern Languages candidates.

While I thoroughly enjoyed my last terms at Repton, I disapproved of the public school system. Above all, I disapproved of the absence of female company and while still at Repton strongly advocated coeducation, of which I learnt something through the fact that my sister, Shamrock, was at a coeducational school, St George's, Harpenden, in Hertfordshire. Forty-three years later, in 1970, Repton was taking girls into the Sixth Form, one of the first of the boys' public schools to do so, and from 1992 girls have been taken from the age of thirteen, two new houses having been built to accommodate them.

During my last year at Repton, I was able with impunity to express my scorn for such things as football matches and for the compulsory standing on the touchline and keeping up a steady roar. I showed what I felt about it by joining another boy in a knit-in. We both knitted scarves while standing on the touchline. To the credit of the school, nobody took the slightest notice of us.

I also let it be known that I was glad to have learnt something of the military training of the British, Ireland's traditional enemy, in case I should ever have to take up arms against them, but that I was not going any further with the training once I had been to camp. That was of course nonsense, but nobody cared. The mood about the corps was changing. There were then already a few, very few, able-bodied boys who never joined the corps, and a year or two after I left, scouting flourished as an alternative to the corps.

In the 1927 Michaelmas Term I did a very silly thing. The classrooms in Repton were scattered. The masters stayed in them and we moved from one to the other, with our straw hats on. The winter uniform was morning coat and striped trousers (I can still wear my last school morning coat for weddings, if required!) and a straw boater with a ribbon on it in one's house colours. One day somebody handed me a paper hat, like one out of a cracker, and dared me to wear it, instead of my boater. Idiotically, I accepted the dare. This was an unbelievably childish thing to do, for we were serious-minded grown men, and I had to walk past the Head and a group of masters standing around him in the school yard. He called me over, told me to take off the hat and to report to him in his study after supper.

I spent an unhappy day thinking what he was going to do to me and what a fool I had been. When I entered his study, he said something like this: 'Well, Trench, I think you and the school have given each other all you have to give. You have passed your exams and have got your place in Cambridge and you are going to study Modern Languages. I do not like boys to leave before the end of the school year; but in your case I think you might profit by going to France or Germany for the rest of the year. See what you can do about that.' That was it! Not a word about the paper hat. He then asked me about life in Ireland and what contact I had with Roman Catholics. He would of course have said that he was a Catholic, but not a Roman Catholic. I am ashamed now to say that my answer was that I did not think that I ever met any Roman Catholics except our servants! 'That is because you live within the Pale', he said.

I was tremendously elated with the Head's suggestion of my going abroad and my father immediately agreed. Plans were made for me to go to Germany to attend lectures at the University of Frankfurt-am-Main.

Fisher left Repton in 1932 and became Bishop of Chester. He was then Bishop of London throughout World War II. He became Archbishop of Canterbury in 1945. In 1961 he retired and was given a life peerage as Baron Fisher of Lambeth. In April of that year he came to Dublin and took part in a service in St Patrick's Cathedral on the occasion of a meeting of the British Council of Churches. I went along with my eldest son, Fiachra, The cathedral was packed to capacity, but when the service was over and the congregation started to move out, I told Fiachra, greatly to his embarrassment, that I was going to speak to Fisher.

When the cathedral was cleared, I waited in the south aisle and presently saw Fisher and Lady Fisher approaching, with George Simms, the Archbishop of Dublin. I did not know what I was going to say, but I stood in their path and as they approached I hailed Fisher with *Floreat Repandunum* — this was not exactly the school motto, but one saw it in use, though I never heard it said. 'Whom have we here?' Fisher asked with his characteristic laugh. He had a phenomenal memory and I dare say he would have identified me, but George Simms gave him my name. After suitable greetings, I turned to Lady Fisher and told her who I was — she was hard of hearing. 'My husband was very fond of you', she said. Considering the thousands of boys who had been through his hands, and all that had happened in the thirty-five years since I had left Repton, I was amazed at this comment. I have always regretted that I never thanked Fisher for that splendid piece of advice he gave me — and which some people have taken to mean that I was expelled!

I do not know whether Fisher was aware that during my last term at Repton I had broken one of the great taboos by making friends outside my own year and enjoying the friendship and the love of a boy two years younger than myself. When I left after this one term of friendship and went to Germany, Bobbie wrote to me every day. Dr Sander, the schoolmaster with whom I was staying, became alarmed at the number of letters I was receiving from the one hand and had the audacity to open one of my letters, acting, he said, *in loco parentis*. He found nothing but a photograph of a very good-looking boy and a letter full of chat about school life. Bobbie did tell me later that Fisher had spoken to the school about the new phenomenon of 'romantic friendships' which had sprung up. He said that this must stop. This resulted in the big boys taking to caning the little boys again, as was done in earlier generations.

During my first term at Cambridge, Bobbie persuaded me to come over to Repton to see him. That visit was not a great success and we drifted apart; but about twelve years later he wrote to me in much distress. He had become a practising homosexual and was very worried. That was a distressful thing to be in the 1930s, though it was clearly his nature, and he looked to me for support or comfort which I was unable to give him, because I found the subject wholly distasteful. Bobbie was then caught up in the war and I never heard of him again, except to be told that he was killed in a car crash in 1970.

As to homosexual activity in public schools, I can only say that I was entirely unaware of any at the Hall, where we slept in open dormitories of about twenty beds. Visiting teams to other schools where they had to stay overnight brought back tales of what could only be described as male prostitution, but I was never on close terms with any team members and do not know whether the tales were well founded.

At Cambridge, almost none of my friends were public-school men and from the time I left Repton, apart from that visit to see Bobbie, I never met any of my contemporaries, at Cambridge or elsewhere, with a single exception. That was Bill Pochin, with whom I made friends for Sunday walks from our first term at Repton. He came over to Ireland in September 1927, that is to say at the very end of my last summer holidays from Repton. He stayed with us at Balnagowan, the house my father had bought in 1925 in Palmerston Park, Dublin, and we went on a bicycle tour of Wicklow. We spent the first night at the Reservoir Cottage, up the

Balnagowan, Palmerston Park, Dublin, the Trench famiy home, 1925–28. Built by a Scot named Smith, hence the name *Baile an ghabhann,* or Smithstown. Like a mini Scottish baronial castle, with a lighthouse on top and the walls battered to withstand the beating of the waves! Later it became a Benedictine students' residence and is now divided into apartments.

steep Killakee Hill. Gerard Crofts and his wife were living there. Gerard was a singer who was well known in nationalist circles. He had taken part in the 1916 Rising and had been in jail where he had contracted a skin ailment from which he never recovered He always wore white cotton gloves to hide his disfigured hands and to protect his skin. He made a living travelling around and singing at concert parties in aid of Sinn Féin funds and the like. He was the first person I made friends with who had been active in 'the movement' and this had a certain fascination for me, though I do not remember him talking about it.

I was already quite familiar with the Killakee area and with Loch Bray and Mrs McGurk's cottage, where she supplied teas. Paddy must have been well known there, for as soon as I said I was his brother, Mrs McGurk produced 'some hitherto not forthcoming very good home-made jam' according to my journal of the tour. The next night we spent in a cottage over the Lower Lake of Glendaloch. We disputed the charge of five shillings each for bed and breakfast and got it reduced to 3s. 6d. for the two of us! The man of the house, Paddy Byrne, had worked in the lead mines at the head of the glen, and talked to us at length about coal and gold and silver and every other kind of mine and produced a book containing the half–year accounts in full detail of every mine in Ireland in the last century.

Next morning we climbed to the top of Lugduff (2,154 feet), back down to Mrs Byrne and away with us on our bikes to the far end of Glenmalure, of which remote spot Paddy had spoken with enthusiasm. There we found an unoccupied house, with a window we could open. It was partly furnished and we spent a night there on two bedsteads with all our clothes on. We found evidence that the owner had been there quite lately.

It belonged to Dr Kathleen Lynn, who had taken part in the Rising as medical officer to Countess Markievicz's battalion in St Stephen's Green. She and the Countess were among seventy women taken prisoner. When released, they were both elected to the executive of Sinn Féin, and no doubt the house in Glenmalure had played its part in the independence movement. In 1955 it was bequeathed by Dr Lynn to An Óige, the Irish Youth Hostel Association, which still runs it as a weekend and summertime youth hostel.

From Glenmalure we went to Avoca, Arklow, Rathnew and Ashford. To visit Walpole's gardens at Mount Usher we should have had a 'member's ticket' — member of what I do not know — but mention of Father's name gained us admittance.

After that our route was up the Devil's Glen, Newtownmount-kennedy, Great Sugar Loaf (top of), Enniskerry, Powerscourt Waterfall, zig-zag to the top gate onto the old Calary Bog road, Roundwood Park (where Mr and Miss Fitzpatrick gave us quantities of bread and honey, and where I had apparently visited on two previous occasions), back to Mrs Byrne's, over the Wicklow Gap, Blessington (where we were warmly welcomed by Brophy, the postman of my early childhood, and his wife, who had been our cook), Kilbride, Glenasmole, and home. Total 200 miles exactly. This whole tour, especially on the rough mountain roads with virtually no traffic and not a house nor a person to be seen for many miles, was far more exciting and adventurous then than any comparable journey would be now.

Bill Pochin did his 'First Med' exam at Repton and the next time he came to Ireland, in the 1950s, he stayed in rather greater comfort at the Shelbourne Hotel for a medical conference. I took him home to Drogheda, where we lived in a house which had formerly been the Blue School and which Bill admired as the sort of place he would like to own when he was much better off. He could not have imagined the small outlay we had on the place and the small income that enabled us to live there. He was knighted in 1975 and became Sir Edward Pochin, having distinguished himself in the field of radiological protection. He died in 1990, aged 80.

A friend said to me that she would like to send her son to an English public school because he was 'definitely public-school material'. I wondered what this could mean and what we had in common which made us 'public-school material'. I decided that the only common denominator was the ability of our parents or guardians to pay the fees.

The earliest year for which I have been able to assertain the fees is 1939 and it is understood that they had not been changed much in the previous twenty years. The figure in 1939 was £177 per annum. It covered tuition, boarding, chapel, sanatorium, library, medical attendance and games. There was a reduction for sons of clergy and for any boy who had a younger brother in the school.

IV

Germany in the 1920's

On 1 January 1928, just five weeks after my eighteenth birthday, I left Balnagowan and started on the first of seven journeys to Germany in the next nine years, specifically in 1928 to Frankfurt-am-Main. First to London, whence it should have been a sixteen-hour journey to Frankfurt. There was a delay somewhere, I missed the connection and had to send a telegram from Köln railway station to my hosts in Frankfurt. The telegram was in impeccably grammatical German, and entirely unidiomatic, as nobody, of course, had taught me German telegraphese, nor thought to enlighten me when I handed it in. In the course of this transaction I saw for the first time the evidence of British occupation of the Rhine and I took an immediate and lasting dislike to what I saw.

For the first two months of my time in Frankfurt I stayed with Oberstudienrat Dr G.H. Sander, who taught English in the Frankfurter Musterschule, or Model School. I had made his acquaintance when he visited Repton in the previous year and had conducted the senior class in German for a time. He lived quite comfortably with his wife and some small children and they did their best to make me feel at home; but I think they found me rather difficult to deal with. I was very bad at making conversation, not only in German, and I coined the phrase *'Ich schweige in allen Sprachen* — I am silent in all languages'.

In spite of this, Sander invited me after a few weeks to join him on a school outing. He was taking his class of about twenty fifteen-year olds away for a few days in the Taunus Mountains, to the north of Frankfurt. We went on a short train journey and then started walking up through the forest. We spent each night in a *Jugendherberge* and that was my introduction to what from 1929 on were known as youth hostels. I was very impressed with the whole concept of the *Jugendherberge* and of this sort of excursion taking place during term time as part of the school curriculum. On one of our day's walks we reached the top of the Grosser Feldberg, the highest mountain in the Taunus range, 2,899 feet, and there was, as usual in Germany, a restaurant at the top. It had a piano, at which I sat down and played a short piece. On being asked by some of the boys if this was something Irish, I thought it best to say yes, rather than to admit that they had failed to recognize my rendering of a piece from Schumann's *Carnaval.*

Apart from Dr Sander, my only other contact in Germany before my arrival there, was my father's aunt, known to us as Aunt Zinnie and to her German nephews and nieces as Tante Helen. She was the reason for our thinking of Frankfurt in the first place, for she had been living there since she had married Moritz von Bernus in 1874.

Uncle Moritz came of a very wealthy family of silk merchants, who had migrated from Italy to Frankfurt in the seventeenth century. Moritz, born in 1843, had some commercial training in London and Paris, with a view to taking over his father's business, but he decided instead to enter the church. He studied theology, but he was unable to take on parochial duties as he suffered badly all his life from asthma. So he was never ordained, but served the church in a different way. In 1881 he built and endowed, out of his own resources, a church in the northern outskirts of Frankfurt, the Christus-Kirche. It still stands and is run as an ecumenical centre in which Moritz's grandnephew, Lex, plays an active part. For health reasons, Moritz and Aunt Zinnie regularly spent the winter in Italy, and Moritz was largely responsible for the building, between 1896 and 1904, of four churches in Italian resorts frequented by Germans. For the Christus-Kirche and the services in Italian and other resorts he devised a special liturgy, based on the Church of England liturgy, with hymns ancient and modern. The services still operate, but the *Verein zur Einrichtung deutsch-evangelischer Gottesdienste in Kurorten,* founded by Moritz and presided over by him, was wound up in 1991.

After completing his church building, Moritz turned to building a summer residence for himself, carving a piece out of the forest outside the village of Falkenstein-im-Taunus. This was the Schardau so beloved of his nephews and nieces and later generations, both Irish and German. For he and Aunt Zinnie had no children, but kept open house for the descendants of his brother, and of her brothers.

The family had for many generations owned a Schloss, or castle, which stands on the Schlossstrasse at the western side of the city of Frankfurt. Aunt Zinnie always used the diminutive form and called it the Schlösschen, to bring it down in size. When I was there, the Schlösschen belonged to Uncle Moritz's nephew, Alexander von Bernus, a widower, who lived there with his daughter, *'die grosse Bettina'*, and his two sons, Olu (since died) and Lex, all born about 1910–12. Alexander was known as Herr Landrat, meaning that he was the administrative officer of a district under the old Prussian system. He did not get on well either with Aunt Zinnie or his own family, and Aunt Zinnie avoided contacts with him.

Uncle Moritz died in 1914 and on the outbreak of war Aunt Zinnie put all his available funds into German war bonds, so that when the collapse came she lost the lot. She lived on the sale of her jewellery and eventually on an annuity which my father organized for her. She had to give up her town house and Herr Landrat let her have the use of a wing of the Schlösschen, which was divided off from the main building and had a separate entrance. She paid her nephew a small rent, the only note of which I have is from her meticulously kept household accounts in the inflation time. These show that she paid him a month's rent of 78,915,000,000,000 marks, which was just about five pounds sterling. She was fortunate to be able to obtain some sterling by the sale of her pearls, with Father's help. She spent the last years of her life entirely at Schardau and died there in 1934, having lived in Frankfurt or neighbourhood for exactly sixty years.

The Schlösschen was very convenient to the University, which I had entered in the middle of the winter semester, and when the semester came to an end on 15 March, I took the opportunity to leave the Sanders and to accept Aunt Zinnie's offer to reside in her wing of the Schlösschen, with an old retainer of hers, Frau Hahn, to 'do' for me. During the four-and-a-half months from then until the end of July I was only inside Herr Landrat's front door once. I had virtually no contact with him and little with his family.

I had enrolled at the university when it reopened on 8 January 1928 after the Christmas break. I attended lectures in German literature and some in French, and I was admitted to a 'Proseminar', a small group sitting round a table with Prof. Dr Sommerfeld, for *Literaturhistorische Uebungen,* or exercises in literary history, Gottfried Keller and C.F. Meyer being the subjects for the winter semester and Hölderlin for the summer semester. This was a great experience for me, though the discussions were rather over my head, even when my knowledge of the language improved. I was by years younger and less mature than the other students.

I seldom ate in the students' canteen and as time was not an important consideration I generally took the tram into the Altstadt, the medieval part of Frankfurt, which I loved and where I had lunch by myself in one simple Wirtshaus or another. Writing about it at the time, I noted that I would pay the equivalent of eightpence for a two-course lunch, the canteen lunch was sixpence, and my student's card entitled me to a tram fare of a penny-halfpenny from any one place in the city to any other.

Through Sommerfeld's seminar I met the only two students, one male, one female, who ever asked me into their own homes or with whom I had any contact outside the university classes. Lore was the only one with whom I established any sort of friendship, whom I took to Schardau without any fear of her being found unacceptable by Aunt Zinnie, and whom I met again in later years. That was a lack on my part, that I did not have those interesting political discussions with other students, which I should have had, and I regretted it afterwards.

In 1928 Hitler had not been heard of. This was the Weimar

Republic and I became enamoured of this social-democratic state. I did pick up, and adopt, German views on the iniquities of the Versailles Treaty, and of the reparations, which appeared to be planned to go on for ever, and on the War Guilt Lie, on which the Treaty of Versailles was based. On the subject of War Guilt I prepared a lengthy paper in February 1931 which I was invited to deliver to one of the undergraduate societies in Cambridge.

When I moved into Aunt Zinnie's wing of the Schlösschen, I spent a great deal of time on my own, and at Aunt Zinnie's piano, and I played through a volume of Beethoven's sonatas, leaving out all the more difficult parts.

At this time I find that I was known as Teddy. My first name, Chalmers, was constantly an embarrassment to me in my early years. I was generally called Chal, and was often told that there was no such name and that I must mean Hal. Fortunately, at prep school and public school I was known by my surname only. Father was aware of my embarrassment and sometimes called me Teddy, my second name being Edward, my mother's father's name. It was a bit surprising that I should have been given a name which might cause me difficulties, as Father was embarrassed by his own first name, Wilbraham, pronounced Wilbra'm in two syllables, not three; but he too would have been known all his life by his surname. I never knew anyone to call him by his first name, except his immediate family who all called him Wil. Mother, who no doubt was keen on the connection with Chalmers, her grandfather, would have been entirely unaware of any possible embarrassment.

Anyway, it appears that in 1928 I was calling myself Teddy. When I came home and mixed more with Gerard Crofts and others in the nationalist tradition, they said, more or less in jest, that they did not think they could associate with anyone called Teddy, so it was decided to call me Terry, by which name I have been most commonly known ever since.

At about the time when my winter semester ended, Aunt Zinnie took an Easter break at one of her favourite resorts, namely Meran in the South Tirol. It had been in Austria when she was there previously, but since 1919 it was in Italy and had become Merano, which Aunt Zinnie greatly deplored, though she loved Italy proper and the Italian language. She invited me to join her in Meran. For shorter rail journeys I always travelled fourth class, in carriages with an open floor space (seats only at either end), for the reception of market baskets, live animals, young trees, or anything else, but for this twelve-hour journey the best I could do was third class. I broke the journey at Innsbruck and loved the view of the Alps rising as it were from the end of the street.

When we reached the Italian frontier, the black-shirted fascisti came along the train for customs and pasport control. My carriage was full and all the passengers were German or Austrian. As each passport was handed up it was stamped automatically and handed back without a word; but I had a British passport and when the officer saw it he bowed to me, stamped it very carefully, bowed again and said, *Grazie, signore,* as he handed it back. My fellow passengers remarked to each other on the special treatment given to the *Engländer,* and I felt so ashamed I promised myself I would never again travel with a British passport.

The reason why I had a British passport was that when I first applied to the Department of External Affairs in Dublin I wrote from Repton and they replied that since I was resident in England I must apply to the British Passport Office. I objected that I was not resident in England, only temporarily incarcerated there, but my objection was over-ruled, so I got my British passport. The next year I suppressed it and got an Irish passport; but three years later I was in London on my way to the Netherlands when I realized that I had forgotten my passport and had to apply to the Irish High Commissioner in London for a temporary one. My travelling companion, Colm O Lochlainn, was a personal friend of the High Commissioner and so I was dealt with without delay; but it was a British passport I was given.

I had a lovely time in Meran. I was in a separate pension from Aunt Zinnie. My fellow guests were all German speaking and were all much older than myself except for one younger woman with whom I made friends — to the extent that I took her to meet Aunt Zinnie. Aunt Zinnie was of course unfailingly polite. *'Aber sie ist keine*

Dame', she said, when Käthe departed — 'but she is not a lady'. She was in fact a telephonist from Berlin.

Meran is about 1,000 feet above sea level and was very beautiful that Easter time, with the fruit trees in blossom. When I left, I did one of the finest mountain walks I have ever done. I took the cable car up another 2,500 feet and remained up at about that height while I walked the twenty miles to Bozen or Bolzano. The few people I met up there were Italian speaking. Meran was largely germanophone but the people were required, for instance, to change the names on gravestones so as to Italianize them.

My sister, Shamrock, was studying music, piano and singing at Hochs Konservatorium in Frankfurt and her time overlapped with mine; but we went our separate ways and did not see much of each other. When we first met it was in the railway station where one or other of us had just arrived. She was pleased to see me and greeted me with a cheerful cry of 'Up the Republic!' That then became our standard greeting. Photographs show that she was with me at Schardau on at least one occasion, and I did meet some of her friends, male and female, not all of whom would have met with Aunt Zinnie's approval, which may be one reason why she was not a more frequent visitor to Schardau.

I was with her on at least one memorable occasion in the Stadion, the great park and outdoor recreation centre outside Frankfurt. We were taking our ease on the grass when we saw a small crowd of people approaching, headed by a man in the uniform of an Irish army officer. We ran towards him, with cries of 'Up the Republic!' for we realized that it was Col. James Fitzmaurice, of the Irish Army Air Corps. With him were Capt. Koehl and Baron von Huenefeld, North-German Lloyd Shipping Company's publicity manager, with whom he had completed the first east to west flight across the Atlantic, from Baldonnel airfield to an island off Labrador. That thirty-six-hour flight, in a plane named 'Bremen', provided by North-German Lloyd, took place on 12–13 April 1928.

At the Uni, the Whit break in 1928 was from 26 May to 2 June, and I planned to cycle to Rothenburg-ob-der-Tauber, in Bavaria, enthusiastically recommended by my fellow student Lore as the most perfectly preserved medieval town in Germany. My route took me twenty miles due south of Frankfurt to Darmstadt and thence through the full length of the Odenwald, a wooded mountainous region stretching from there about fifty miles to Heidelberg. In the forest, at the end of a steep track inaccessible to motor traffic, I visited the Odenwaldschule.

I see from my diary of this tour that I had two friends in the Odenwald School, a young chemistry master and a girl pupil. The master was a friend of Shamrock's and secured a room for me in the farm-house where he was living. I had meals with the school, where visitors were common. I was very impressed with the freedom and informality of this international coeducational school and with its headmaster, Paul Geheeb, addressed by all as Paulus or Saint Paul, because of his beard and saintly appearance.

Geheeb was the subject of a monograph, *Paul Geheeb et la libre communauté scolaire de l'Odenwald: une expérience moderne d'éducation,* published in 1923 by the Bureau International des Écoles Nouvelles, Geneva. One thing which evidently attracted my attention, for I have underlined it, is a reference to *le bain d'air,* which consisted of fifteen minutes of gym in the nude every morning before breakfast on a playing field at the edge of the forest. Definitely not a Repton tradition! The boys went first and the girls later.

From the Odenwaldschule I rode on to Heidelberg. Before leaving Frankfurt I had paid the equivalent of sixpence for a youth hostel card and I stayed in the Heidelberg youth hostel for an overnight charge of twopence. It was Whit Sunday, the town was crowded with visitors and there was a great display that night of fireworks and the illumination of the castle and the bridge across the river Neckar.

Next morning, I set off at seven o'clock and rode up the Neckar valley for thirteen hours, according to my diary, no doubt at a leisurely pace, through many pretty villages, when towards eight o'clock p.m. I had an accident with a pick-up truck full of people returning home from the Whitsun festivities in Heidelberg. Like everyone I had met in Heidelberg (but not in Frankfurt) they were very friendly — rather too friendly and anxious to help me on my way by giving me a tow, with the result that I fell off and cut my arms and legs rather badly on the stony road. I still have the scars on my right hand and left forearm. So bike and I were carried on the truck for another fifteen miles and were deposited at the municipal hospital of Heilbronn and that was as far as I ever got on the road to Rothenburg.

A feature of life in the Weimar Republic which I appreciated was a general feeling of freedom and of informality in personal relations. I might equally well have found this elsewhere. It was in any case a great change from the restrictions of boarding-school.

The formality and comfort of Aunt Zinnie's earlier life in Germany had given way to a 'levelling' which she found 'salutory'. She felt she had been too comfortable. But after the war and the inflation the change was of course much more drastic, though she did manage to retain one servant in Schardau and the old housekeeper in the Schlösschen. She also had her niece, Aileen Trench, staying with her. Aileen had trained as a professional gardener and was a rare sight in Dublin — a lady in breeches.

Aunt Zinnie found me rather too informal on my visits on week-ends to Schardau, wearing nothing in the warmer weather but shorts, sandals, and an open-necked shirt. I heard from home that she would prefer me to show more respect to her in the matter of dress. I had the greatest respect and affection for her and would not willingly have done anything to offend her, so from then on I continued to wear my shorts for the walk up to Schardau, but I carried a pair of trousers to change into.

Schardau was a splendid house, built by Uncle Moritz in English Tudor style, but it fitted very well into the German countryside. It was half-timbered like most of the houses in Falkenstein and neighbourhood. It contained some beautiful furniture, some of it embellished with Aunt Zinnie's *petit point* and it was full of books in French and Italian as well as English and German. It was very much a cultured abode of the late Victorian/Edwardian era.

Aunt Zinnie still played at the piano and sang. And her German relations were of the same cultured and civilized nature. So it was with some amusement that Aunt Zinnie used to recount a story of the French occupation. Frankfurt and Falkenstein were in the French occupied zone after the war and Schardau itself had been occupied by French officers. Aunt Zinnie had suffered much humiliation rather than depradation. Her obvious association with the Allied Powers, and her fluency in French, made no difference. She was the hated and defeated enemy. She asked some soldiers, *'Pourquoi vous êtes ici, croyez-vous?'* and received the reply, *'Pour civiliser les allemands'*, which Aunt Zinnie thought very ironic.

My university term ended at the end of July, and I spent the month of August cycling down the Rhine on my way home.

Frau Hahn gave me some sandwiches to take with me and she apologized for having spread the margarine on both sides of the sandwich. There was no butter, because all Germany's butter had to be exported for 'reparations'. Frau Hahn excused herself for the gross extravagance of spreading both sides by saying, *'Aber es klebt besser zusammen* — but it sticks together better'. Many times since then I have found myself saying, when making sandwiches, *Aber es klebt besser zusammen.*

My tour started with an hour's train journey and a seven-hour walk through the Taunus to Wiesbaden, where I picked up my bike. I was 'much distressed' to see that the royal castle was now known as Connaught Barracks and was swarming with khaki. Perhaps the Duke of Connaught was colonel of the resident regiment.

The youth hostel in Wiesbaden was full and I shared a room in an inn for that night. Next night, in contrast, I was alone in the youth hostel of Bad Schwalbach, which was largely ruined and in what I noted at the time was a 'revolting state' as the result of French occupation, from which it had not yet recovered. The French occupying forces had by this time withdrawn from points further east, but the British were still in occupation of much of the Rhine valley. I did quite a lot of walking as well as cycling, down the Rhine and its tributaries, the Lahn and the Mosel, and in the Eifel hills to the Laacher See, and on down the Rhine again to Düsseldorf, and I stayed in twenty-five different places, twenty of them being youth hostels, from the very primitive to the fairly comfortable.

V

Cambridge

In October 1928 I entered Cambridge University as a member of Sidney Sussex College. Sidney was founded in 1596 and was thus the youngest of the seventeen colleges in the university, except for Downing College, which was founded more than two hundred years later. It was also one of the smallest, having about 175 students in residence, whether undergraduates or postgraduate. The buildings were of a rich red brick, pleasant to look at, and I was very happy to be there. Its most famous member, before I entered, was Oliver Cromwell, of whom the famous 'warts and everything' portrait hangs in the dining-hall. It is a small portrait in crayons and is protected by a curtain on a rail, which I used to pull aside for the benefit of any Irish visitors, that they might express their views on the subject, should they so wish.

I was entered for the Modern and Medieval Languages Tripos, which is what the examination for honours degrees is called, my chosen languages being German and French. My German professor was Karl Breul, Ph.D. (Berlin), who had been living in England since the early years of the century, but was interned during the 1914–18 war as an enemy alien. He was the compiler of the 1906 and 1909 editions of Cassell's German and English Dictionary, still current in the 1920s, and he soon discovered that I was in some ways better informed than he was on current German usage and vocabulary and he was glad to receive from me a number of corrections and suggestions for the new edition on which he was working.

He also made me librarian of the Beit Library. This was the German Students Library, established in 1913 by Otto Beit, father of the late Sir Alfred Beit, of Russborough, County Wicklow. I was paid two shillings an hour for cataloguing and reorganizing the library, which I loved doing. That is how I come to have a German–English Commercial Dictionary with the Beit Library bookplate in it. Prof. Breul told me to take it when a new edition came in.

The Tripos examination was divided into two parts. Part I was taken at the end of one's first year and was an examination in two languages — translation from and into the chosen languages, essay, and oral. I passed this with first class honours in German, second class in French and a 'distinction' in the oral exam in both languages. The College had awarded me an Exhibition, that is to say, a contribution towards fees, on the result of the Entrance Scholarship Examination which I had sat for in December 1927, and now gave me a book prize, which I spent on books on Irish history and current affairs. The five volumes bear the arms of Sidney Sussex College.

Part II consisted of an exam in five subjects, selected from a list of fifty-seven possibilities, plus an essay in one of the languages chosen, bearing on the history and civilization of the country concerned. The normal thing was to take either all five subjects relating to one language, or three relating to one and two to another.

During my first year I developed a passionate desire to do Irish in my remaining years, but there was no Department of Celtic Studies in Cambridge and Irish was not catered for in the Modern and Medieval Languages Tripos. I made enquiries, but first of all I knew nothing about literature in the Irish language, so I wrote to Father about this. He got Douglas Hyde, Professor of Modern Irish in the National University of Ireland, to write me a letter about the importance of this literature, and armed with this I approached, as I was instructed, the Head of the Department of Other Languages — other, that is, than the ten covered by the Modern and Medieval Languages Tripos. This turned out to be O.H.P. Prior, Professor of French, with whom I got on well and who had conducted the

French oral exam in a very friendly way, congratulating me on *l'affinité celtique.* He was sympathetic, but the best he could suggest was that I should do Irish under the Archaeological and Anthropological Tripos, Section B. This section was headed 'Anglo-Saxon and kindred subjects', and the kindred subjects included 'The Celtic Peoples' and the Irish language. So Prior directed me to H.M. Chadwick, Professor of Anglo-Saxon, who said to me, 'If you want to study Old Irish, I shall have to teach you; but I'd much rather teach you Sanskrit!'

I must have acquired some knowledge of Irish before I went to Germany, or at least an introduction to the language. I think that must mean that I had already in 1927 had a preliminary lesson from Máire Ní Néill, Bean Uí Mhurchadha, or Mary Murphy, and I think it was she who told me of George Thomson in Cambridge, whom I now went to see. He was an Englishman and a classics Fellow of King's College, Cambridge. He had been many times to the Blasket Islands and spoke and wrote Irish with fluency. However, he was not interested in teaching me Irish and could not help me in that respect. (I shall have more to say about him in Chapter VIII.)

So there was nothing for me to do but to concentrate on Part II of the Modern and Medieval Languages Tripos, in which I elected to do three German subjects and two French.

In the long summer vacation 1929 I stayed with a French family for a while at St Aubin-sur-Mer, about sixteen miles from Dieppe. It was a Parisian family, comfortably off, who, typically, owned or rented a nice big house by the sea where they spent the summer, and indeed other times too, and took in foreign visitors. It was quite a lot of fun and I enjoyed the company of the eldest daughter, Kate, and her friends.

I met Kate again next year when I went to Paris for an Easter vacation course at the Institut Britannique where we had lectures from visiting Sorbonne professors and were able to read in the Bibliothèque Nationale. I must have been interested in art history, for my thesis was the life and work of Ingres.

I heard from Kate again in February 1931, when she wrote to me on the printed letter heading of Le Grand Comité de Paris with an impressive list of ministers, ambassadors and members of the Académie Française and others as patrons and Comité d'honneur. I was appointed agent for a beauty queen, Mademoiselle Paris, for whom Kate was organizing a tour of France and abroad for the display of *la haute couture* and a demonstration of the exercises and make-up used by the young *parisienne soucieuse de la beauté de ses lignes.* However, before I completed negotiations for a suitable venue in Cambridge I was sent a newspaper cutting saying that Mlle Paris had been discovered to be not *une jeune fille cent pour cent,* because she had a baby a few months old and she had been deposed. That was the beginning and end of my career as an impresario.

I had before this dabbled in acting to a very small extent, but it did lead to my appearing on the stage of the Abbey Theatre with Orson Welles! Firstly, I got involved with Shamrock's dalliance with the stage. I have a handbill, with a design by Harry Kernoff, which declares that Shamrock Trench presents, for the first time in Dublin, *A Wedding* by John Kirkpatrick and *Fortunato* by Quintero, at the Peacock Theatre, on three nights in September 1929. The programme gives Mary Manning as the producer of *A Wedding,* in which I played the part of the groomsman, and Shamrock as the producer of *Fortunato,* in which I played the part of a blind man with a fiddle. I also apparently had the job of collecting the dues for the dozen or so advertisements in the programme, including one sum of 14s. 6d. 'paid by WFT' evidently for an ad which I had failed to collect. My fellow actors included A.J Leventhal, a friend and contemporary of my brother Paddy in TCD and of Samuel Beckett. Leventhal became an assistant to the Professors of French and German.

I used in those days to wear an open-necked shirt and a floppy bow tie. 'He looks like Lord Byron', said someone to my father. 'Oh no', said Father, 'Byron was quite a good-looking man.'

I appeared for a whole week in the Abbey Theatre in 1931, in a production by Madeleine Ross, when the Abbey Theatre company was away in America. The *Evening Mail* of 3 December noted: 'Mr Teiri Trench, who is appearing at the Abbey Theatre in

Mr Somerset Maugham's delightful comedy *The Circle,* is comparatively new to the Dublin audience, having gained most of his experience in the German Society in Cambridge. But he will be seen under exceptionally favourable circumstances in this production, as the cast is an extremely strong one, including Miss Blanaid O'Carroll, Mr Tom Purefoy, and Mr Orson Welles, who has been appearing in the recent productions at the Gate Theatre'. And *Model Housekeeping* of January 1932 picked me out for special mention as 'very promising'. Promising or not, that was the end of my acting career, but not, I believe, of Orson Welles's. My recollection of him is of a fat overgrown schoolboy. He was in fact sixteen years old, but had somehow brazened himself onto the Gate Theatre stage.

The career I had in mind for myself from the time I left school was teaching. I remember Prof. Breul asking his class of over one hundred undergraduates what they intended to do, and his disappointment that only two of us thought of teaching. Most of the others, it seems to me, were heading for the civil or diplomatic service. I was determined to live and work in Ireland and Father was doubtful if I would find teaching a rewarding experience. He thought I should talk it over with the secretary of the Department of Education. This was JJ, or Joseph, O'Neill, author of *Land Under England,* an allegorical fantasy, for which AE wrote a foreword when it was first published in 1935.

O'Neill was born on the Aran Islands, son of a Royal Irish Constable. He went to Queen's College, Galway, and was a student of Father's, for whom he had a great admiration and Father regarded him as perhaps his most interesting student. He became a school inspector and finally secretary of the Department. I called on him in his office in Hume Street and he invited me to come to his weekly soirée, where one never knew who might turn up. I went there on 21 September 1929. We were alone together for a time and we talked about life in England and life in Ireland. O'Neill found society in England more interesting 'because there are so few here with whom you can discuss things — like Dr [Bob] Collis, and your father, with whom I used to have such interesting discussions'.

AE came in and O'Neill asked him if he was always optimistic about this country. He replied that he had a certain optimism about the universe, and he went on to talk about the Indian theory of cycles, the journal of Countess Tolstoy, the movements of the planets, the physical strength of Tolstoy, of Shelley, and of Shakespeare, and much else, all in one long monologue, with an occasional word from O'Neill to get him going again. I was fascinated and so impressed that when I got home I wrote down everything I could remember of what had been said.

Following on this I also went to W.B. Yeats's weekly soirée. Unfortunately I arrived on the wrong day, which was a bit embarrassing as everyone, but everyone, knew which was Yeats's evening. The great man opened the door himself and very nicely told me to come back the next day. There were a few others there, and I think AE turned up again, but I did not find it as interesting as the previous meeting. Going back to Cambridge a few days after that severed the connection with those soirées and I never resumed that contact. I was not really comfortable at that level of intellectual activity and had nothing to contribute to it myself.

At Cambridge none of the colleges was able to accommodate all its members in rooms in college and most colleges required its undergraduates, except scholars of the house, to spend their first years in licensed lodgings and to reside in college only for their last year or so. In Sidney we did things the other way round, which I found much preferable. One became integrated into the college in one's first year. So on my return in October 1929, I went into 'licensed lodgings'. They were modest enough compared with some I visited, but I was well satisfied with them and stayed at the one address for two years. Cost was an important consideration. I had an annual allowance from Father which as far as I remember was £300, and out of that I paid for everything — initial expenses, fees, board and lodging, personal expenses and travel. I was very pleased with this arrangement and with being entrusted with the entire management of my affairs within this annual figure. And it was just about right, based on average figures given in *The Students' Handbook.*

The Sidney Sussex College Annual for 1928 reveals that of the fifty-six entrants to the college that year, nineteen were from public schools. I note this only because I know that some people think that Cambridge University in those far-off days was peopled almost exclusively by public-school men. Others may have been on county or other scholarships, and some of these had distinguished careers, either academic or in government service.

University and college discipline had some quaint features. Academical dress was required to be worn not only at all lectures and exams and in chapel and dining-hall, but also in the streets after dusk in all parts of the town and neighbourhood. Academical dress meant gown and also the black square cap known as a mortar-board. This enabled undergraduates to be recognized in the streets by the proctors. These were important university officers who had charge of university discipline and who patrolled the streets on foot from time to time accompanied by their two 'bulldogs', brawny men in top hats known to be fast runners. The penalty for breaches of the rules regarding the wearing of the academical dress, was 6s. 8d., being one-third of a pound. It was the duty of the proctors to repress any riotous proceedings in or out of university lodgings, and to prevent students 'from engaging in any pursuits or practices which are objectionable as being cruel, dangerous, liable to produce gambling, inconsistent with gentlemanly behaviour, or detrimental to good order'.

I was only once approached by a proctor, or to be exact by his bulldog, who came forward to me where I was sitting by the river after dusk, and the bulldog told me very politely that the proctor would like to speak to me. I thought perhaps he liked, or disliked, the appearance of my female companion, but it was only to remind me, equally politely, that I should be wearing my mortar-board.

College gates were closed at 10 p.m.; after that hour no one was allowed, without special permission, to leave his college, and the names of students who came after 10 p.m. were recorded. To be out after midnight without leave was a serious breach of discipline. These rules had also to apply to students in lodgings, so lodging-keepers were required to lock doors and windows at 10 p.m. I never found these regulations as burdensome as they now sound.

VI

The German Connection

In Septenber 1929, an Anglo-German Association was formed simultaneously in London and Berlin by prominent persons in both countries, with the aim of promoting general friendly relations between Great Britain and Germany, and to secure a better understanding between the two countries. I felt that there was a need for this in Cambridge and, together with a Scot named Jock Murray, I announced on 15 November 1929 the proposal to form a similar Association in Cambridge, with the official sanction of the London committee and a promise of their support.

I made contact with about a dozen German students in Cambridge and was invited to the first German Evening of the Anglo-German Academic Bureau in London, where it seems to me that the proceedings were conducted entirely in German, though in the following year they were entirely in English. And in the Cambridge University Anglo-German Association, about to be launched, the proceedings would be entirely in English since they were not intended for German speakers, but for anyone interested in discussions on subjects of political or economic interest concerning Britain or Germany.

It was in this connection that I met Dina, with whom I had my first love affair. She was an aristocratic German from the Baltic provinces of the Russian empire, namely from Latvia. Her ancestors were amongst the Teutonic knights who colonized that area in the twelfth century, exactly at the time when the Anglo-

Normans arrived in Ireland. But Father got very cross with me for suggesting that the two were comparable. I think that what upset him was that the German colonists had remained German and never anything else, whereas the Anglo-Normans were completely integrated with the native population, becoming indeed *Hibernicis ipsis hiberniores.* The Baltic provinces were devastated in the 1914–18 war and in the fighting which continued into the 1920s. The nobility were of course expropriated and Dina's home was now in Berlin. She was not a student; she was older than the students and was, I suppose, an au pair, though I think the term was not yet in common use. She was looking after the child of a Russian doctor from the same Baltic province, with the same family name as herself, but without the von which she had to her name. He was a University lecturer in physiology.

When Dina returned to Berlin, she wrote to me asking me to marry her and to join her in Berlin, where she was sure I could earn a living — at what it was not clear and fortunately I had my head screwed on tight, being then aged twenty. On the rebound of receiving my negative reply she married the doctor and went to live with him in Egypt. I next met her in the 1950s in the village of Collon, seven miles north-west of Drogheda, where I was then living. She had become Her Serene Highness, though I doubt she ever used the title, having married a man from, again, the same Baltic province and with the title of a Russian prince, but now English and working in Whitehall.

They were over visiting his relations in Collon, where there had been a small colony of Russian émigrés since the 1920s. During World War Two, officers of the British armed forces or other services who were required to learn Russian were given the choice of Paris or Collon, and a steady flow of them chose Collon. That too is where some senior Irish civil servants learnt Russian.

When I first knew her Dina taught me two phrases of Russian, *Ya liubliú tibiá* (I love you) and *Nié pokidáy miniá* (Do not desert me). I had not much use for these phrases for the next thirty years or more, but then while I was working in Drogheda, I acquired the agency for BN biscuits, of Nantes, for which a stand had been booked in the Food and Wine section of a *Quinzaine Française* in Dublin. I manned the stand for the fortnight and it turned out to be the only food item in the section, all the others being wine. One day an old tramp (or so she looked) came in, very poorly dressed, with her feet out through her broken boots. She came down the line of wine booths and stopped at one, at which I heard her speak in French. So when she reached me we exchanged a few sentences in French, and then I said, *'Mais vous n'êtes pas française, madame'*. *'Non'*, she replied, *'je suis juive russe'*. *'Ya liubliú tibiá'*, said I. *'Nié pokidáy miniá'*. *'Ah'*, she said, *'si j'avais dix-huit ans je vous embrasserais!'* So at least my Russian was understandable after a lapse of some thirty years.

When that *quinzaine* came to an end, I wanted to speak to a certain journalist in the *Irish Times*, so I went to the Pearl Bar in Fleet Street, the recognized place for meeting such people. There sitting at the bar I saw another journalist, Lord Killanin. He was at that time president of the Olympic Council of Ireland and was about to leave for Moscow to take part in the negotiations regarding the proposed holding of the Olympic Games there. I knew that he spoke and wrote French with fluency, and I asked him whether he also spoke Russian. 'No', said he, 'but I understand that you do.' 'Really?' 'Yes', he said, 'you were heard speaking Russian in some public place.'

In January 1930, the Cambridge University Anglo-German Association, of which I was joint Honorary Secretary, was launched at an Inaugural Dinner at which G.P. Gooch, author of many books on modern British and European, especially German, history, proposed the toast of Germany, to which one of the German students responded, namely Karl Kuno Overbeck, of whom I shall have more to say presently.

The other major event of that year, for me, was the production by the Cambridge University German Society of *Die Journalisten*, by Gustav Freytag, of which I can still remember some catch phrases, and in which I played the part of Senden, property owner and editor of a conservative newspaper in the throes of a provincial election. We all appeared with our initials at that time, so I was

C.E.F. Trench. The following year I was Eamonn Trench (Eamonn being a possible Gaelic rendering of Edward) in *Minna von Barnhelm*, a comedy by G.E. Lessing, in which I played the part of Paul Werner, retired sergeant-major, and captured the affections of Minna's maid, Franciska. This was the total of my acting experience in the German Society in Cambridge. This was the society for the students of German, quite different from the Anglo-German Association.

I do not see the name of Henning Thomsen anywhere in my records. He must have been in Cambridge the previous year, 1928–29. He was the only one I knew who bore the *Schmiss* — the scar on his face from student duelling, which I always thought repulsive. He entered the diplomatic service, as many of the Germans at Cambridge did. He came to Dublin in 1938 as First Secretary of the German legation, and remained on during the war. After the war and after the de-nazification process, he was re-instated at the German Foreign Office and was promoted to ambassador rank. He died in 1975.

Approaching the summer of 1930, I decided I must get a holiday job to see me through the long vacation, and I applied to Lunn's Tours for a job as a courier. I went up to London for interview and got the job. I was given three instructions. One, pay particular attention to the oldest and to the least attractive of the females in the party which you are conducting, and make a point of dancing with them. Two, do not accept the resultant invitation to go up to her room to look at family photographs. Three, on and from the first day of the vacation be prepared to go anywhere at a moment's notice. This meant that I would not necessarily be sent to any country of which, or of whose language, I had any knowledge.

When I told my tutor in Sidney Sussex what I was planning to do, he said that it would be a complete waste of time and if the college gave me a grant to pay my fare, had I somewhere where I could stay in France or Germany? I had. So I got the grant. I think it was £15, twice that sum being the sort of amount one might have paid for a two-week holiday with full board. With this grant I arranged to stay with Aunt Zinnie in Schardau, and also to visit three of my German friends from Cambridge.

Franz Wittwer was not a student but a bookseller. He was

working in a bookshop in Cambridge when I made friends with him and I invited him over to Ireland. I took him over the Wicklow Mountains as a pillion passenger on Father's motor-bike, which he thought a most extraordinary experience, and a most uncomfortable one. We went up Killakee Hill and called in to see Gerard Crofts in his cottage there. Franz, from the sophisticated elegance of Stuttgart, could not understand why anyone should choose to live in such conditions.

Wittwer was the W. H. Smith of southern Germany, with the book-stall concession in all the railway stations. I paid my return visit to him in the summer of 1930. He was back running the business with his father by that time. Though he was as hospitable as could be, I sensed that he was embarrassed to receive a visitor whose only baggage was a rucksack.

I looked round Stuttgart on my own. The tallest building in the city was the tower-house of the *Stuttgarter Neue Tagblatt,* the highest newspaper building in Germany, sixty-one metres high, with a look-out platform on the sixteenth floor, which I duly visited. I took the express lift non-stop to the fifteenth floor, but came down in the paternoster. This was a continuously moving lift with open compartments which one steps into and out of while on the move. It makes a shuffling sound, said to resemble a priest saying his prayers. Hence its name. This was the first one I had seen and I could not make out what the mechanism was which enabled it to carry this series of compartments round the top and again round the bottom to make a continuous circuit. I decided to investigate, knowing for certain that the compartment was not going to collapse, so I got into one of them and stayed in it while it went below the ground floor into the basement and started coming up again. Half way between the basement and the ground floor it stopped. I realized that it was one o'clock p.m. on Saturday, and that it might not move again until Monday. I banged on the walls and jumped up and down and slowly it started to move again. The whole remaining staff in the building were assembled on the ground floor to see what was going on. I passed through them quickly without a word. And I still did not know how it worked!

Two other experiences of that summer of 1930 struck me at the time as being so uniquely interesting that I sent a long report on them to my father and asked to have it returned to me. Here are some extracts in abbreviated form.

On 4 June I arrived in Bonn and was met by Karl Kuno Overbeck, who told me that the Corps Rhenania–Bonn, to which he belonged, was celebrating its 110th anniversary during this week-end. This was one of the many students' societies or fencing clubs which were founded and flourished particularly during and after the uprising of national feeling in Germany in opposition to Napoleon. Some of these corps acquired the reputation of doing nothing but getting drunk, insulting each other and then cutting each other's faces open. Overbeck wanted to show me a different picture of them. Rhenania, to which his father also belonged, was the oldest and most exclusive corps in Bonn.

This was their annual reunion, which was an extra big affair every ten years. I met a number of corps members, distinguished by their colourful caps and sashes, and spent a pleasant and informal evening with them and their girl friends in the garden of a *Weinhaus* overlooking the Rhine, such as I had never had with students in Frankfurt. I learnt a lot about the corps activities, the initiation of new members, and so on, and wrote of this and of the next day's festivities in much detail. For the principal ceremony on the next evening only Rhenaner and other invited corps members were allowed in the big hall, to the number of about two hundred and fifty, and only ladies were allowed in the gallery, plus a brass band at the other end. So Karl Kuno had procured a *Damenkarte* for me on which I appeared as Frau/Frl. Trench, and armed with this priceless pass I joined a few dozen ladies in the gallery, where Karl Kuno's mother explained to me, when necessary, what was going on.

Rhenania–Bonn had its own song-book, and we had nearly two hours of singing, accompanied by the brass band, which also played martial music in the intervals between songs and speeches. The speeches referred naturally to the Rhineland, which had been freed of military occupation only four days previously, to German territories still occupied and to other iniquities of *der Versailler Unfrieden*, the non-Peace Treaty of Versailles; but in my report at the time I regarded them as 'wholly unaggressive'. We had a half-hour of toasts proposed by members representing each semester, from the youngest back to a heavily bearded ninety-year-old. Every item was introduced with the banging of swords on tables by the members presiding at each end of the six long tables, and the rattling of beer mugs. Coming up to midnight, with lights dimmed, we had the most sacred part of the celebrations, common to all German corps, and involving the singing of a patriotic song, *Landesvater*, the beating of swords together and the collecting of the caps on the points of the swords.

The steamer trip next day, from Bonn to Coblenz and back, with colours flying and band playing, was strictly confined to corps members and their ladies, and no exception could be made for me, so I had a swim in the Rhine, as on the previous day, and took the slow train back to Frankfurt. The airship, Graf Zeppelin, accompanied us on part of the journey, a beautiful sight, on her first visit to the freed Rhineland.

Much as I enjoyed the hospitality and the entertainment and the pleasant company in Bonn, I retained a strong antipathy to the principles and practice of the fighting corps. My interest was in the Youth Movement, with which the corps was as much out of sympathy as with the social democrats of the Weimar Republic.

I must have shown my report to Karl Kuno when we met again in Cambridge, for I have a note on it that he marvelled at the minute accuracy of my account of the ceremonial in Bonn; but when he saw the song-book, bearing the monogram and the colours of Rhenania–Bonn, on the mantelpiece in my rooms, he politely asked me to remove it and to regard it as something very special, not to be associated with the fixture cards and invitations of other student societies. I was to understand that I was highly privileged to have been allowed to witness such an occasion.

That year was my last contact with Karl Kuno until, about forty-two years later, my wife Bea received a phone call from the German Embassy enquiring whether her father-in-law had been a student at Cambridge in 1930. No, she said, but her husband was.

Oh, in that case, the new German Ambassador would like to speak to me. This turned out to be Karl Kuno, who immediately on settling in to his new office had asked his secretary to try and trace me. The whole of the Republic of Ireland being covered at that time by two telephone directories made the task easier! I went to dine with Karl Kuno and his family just once and a few months later I returned to the Embassy to sign the book of condolences, for he had dropped dead. I never found out what he had been doing since Cambridge days, except that he and the only other guest at the dinner had been in Greece during the war — in what capacity I do not know.

Just a week after the 110th anniversary of Rhenania–Bonn I attended another anniversary — the 600th anniversary of the first mention in any known record of the village of Rauisch–Holzhausen, about sixty miles north of Frankfurt. I was during that summer vacation of 1930 based in the Schlösschen in Frankfurt and I went up to Schardau as usual on the Friday after the Bonn episode. Two days later I walked the nine miles through the forest to Bad Homburg vor der Höhe and took the train via Giessen and Marburg to the little town of Kirchhain. I had apparently not confirmed the day or time of my arrival and there was no one to meet me, and there was no telephone service on Sunday, so I walked the five miles to Holzhausen, a village of eight hundred inhabitants.

This was the home, or at least the seat, of the von Stumm family, and I had an invitation from Baron Carl von Stumm, known as Carlo. They had an immense castle there in mock English Tudor style, but they had not lived there for some years. I believe that Carlo's father had become *persona non grata* in Germany and lived in Switzerland and that his family had a major interest in the coal mines in the Saar Territory which were ceded to France by the Treaty of Versailles, but what his supposed transgression was I do not know.

I found my way to the baronial castle, standing in splendid parkland. It was kept in good order, but was occupied solely by an old retainer, Herr Wilke, who introduced himself as the *maître d'hôtel.* He prepared a suite of rooms, produced a series of excellent meals for me and Carlo, who joined me there, waited on us at table, and entertained us with endless stories of his ten years with Carlo's grandfather, Imperial German Ambassador to Spain, his twenty-two years with the late King Carol of Rumania, his acquaintance with Kaiser Wilhelm II, and so on. He was a chevalier and he spoke five languages, but no English.

The village of Holzhausen was in festive array, decorated with wreaths and flags and flowers. The tiny village square was surrounded with open refreshment tents full of people drinking beer and there was a make-shift dancing platform and a brass band that played endless waltzes, or accompanied the community singing. The women and girls from Holzhausen and the surrounding villages all wore their regional Hessian dress, which varied according to whether the village was Protestant, in sombre blues and browns, or Catholic, in bright colours, the religion of the village depending on which side the local landlord supported in the Thirty Years War, 1618–48.

After dinner we went back into the village and joined the burgomaster, the von Stumms' agent, Herr Naumann, the village doctor and a group of some twenty or thirty students from Marburg, active members of the Hessen-Preussen corps, of which the doctor was an *alter Herr,* or senior member, and for whom he had provided a barrel of beer — watery, to my taste. We had an entertaining time until two o'clock in the morning.

Next day there was a historical pageant and a two-hour dramatic performance representing three phases of local history — the coming of Christianity, the granting of the land by the Archbishop of Mainz to the Knight of Rau in 1330 and the religious wars and the intervention of the von Raus to protect the villages from the tyranny of the local magistrate and bailiffs. The von Raus remained lords of the manor for nearly 550 years, until they died out and their place was taken in 1873 by von Stumm, Carlo's grandfather. The drama was presented in the natural open-air theatre of the baronial park, which gave ample scope for horses to gallop on and off the stage, while wings and green room were provided by the dense forest, in which a clearing had been made. It was an extraordinarily good performance, by the local people, with a text in verse composed by the leading farmer in the area, who was a student of local history.

That evening Carlo was invited out to dinner at a neighbouring estate, and was driven there in his Victoria carriage with a fine pair of horses. I rejoined Herr Naumann, the burgomaster and the doctor and his group in the village square and before we parted the doctor rose and gave a little speech proposing a toast to Ireland and myself. My reply was somewhat disrupted by Carlo's horses, whipped up to a gallop through the village — *pour épater les bourgeois?*

The castle was built in 1873–76 by Carlo's grandfather and the architect, curiously enough, was Aunt Zinnie's nephew, von Kaufmann, who also designed Schardau. She remembered him expressing annoyance at His Excellency's idea of architecture, which required him to add little towers and excrescences on top of his Tudor mansion. The bedroom suites were beautifully furnished, and we had our meals in one of them because all the other rooms were shut up and covered with dust-sheets; but I had a look around the enormous library, the museum of Spanish and other artefacts, and the dining-room which was so vast that Carlo had never seen it in use. I signed the visitors' book, as the fourth visitor in two years, the same book which Kaiser Wilhelm II signed when he stayed there as Crown Prince (that must have been in 1888).

Carlo and I took the two carriage horses for a two-hour ride of inspection of the estate and Carlo gave me the first riding lesson I had had for several years. I had not ridden for two years, and had never been taught to ride 'correctly', as Carlo now showed me. I think that was probably the last time I ever rode. The estate consisted of 2,000 morgen of forest, 600 morgen of farmland and 400 morgen of parkland, said to be the most beautiful park in Central Germany. The Prussian morgen is about two-thirds of a statute acre. Total say 2,000 acres, or 800 hectares.

We went deer-stalking each evening, with the forester, not to shoot, but to see what might need to be culled. I saw marten and wild cats and woodpeckers and was very excited to see and hear the roe-deer at close quarters for the first time, bellowing, grazing, and galloping past us in our hiding place in the woods.

I have thus condensed twenty-five pages of a handwritten report, seven typed pages and some newspaper cuttings, on what remain for me unique experiences of a bygone age.

My interest in Germany had led me to an acquaintance with Georg von Dehn, the German consul-general in Dublin, who with the opening of a legation in 1929 became the first German Minister to the Irish Free State. I had never found him to be anything but courteous and friendly. Others found him maladroit and tactless and, after a particular blunder on the eve of his departure from Dublin for another posting, he was dismissed from the service in 1934. He was replaced by Herr von Kuhlmann, who was succeeded by Eduard Hempel. Hempel served from 1937 until the collapse of Germany in 1945.

In the summer of 1930 I received a phone call from von Dehn. A group of German youths had arrived, knowing little English, and he wanted someone to look after them and show them something of Dublin before they went on to friends in the west of Ireland. I agreed to meet them and it was arranged that they would phone me immediately from wherever they were in Dublin. This turned out to be a phone booth somewhere about College Green. I told them to walk up Grafton Street, St Stephen's Green West, and Harcourt Street and I would meet them in my car, or to be exact in my father's Fiat tourer, i.e. a large open car or 'convertible'.

By the time I reached the bottom of Harcourt Street I could see the group approaching from the top of Grafton Street. There were four or five of them and they were followed by a crowd of ragged youngsters, with which Dublin abounded at that time. I met up with them at the College of Surgeons and bundled them into the car as quickly as I could and fled from the scene. It was no wonder that they aroused some curiosity for the like had never been seen in Dublin before. They were dressed in military-style uniforms, with long-skirted overcoats of the field-grey colour of the German army. They carried 'tornisters' (military knapsacks) and staves. Rucksacks of any kind were very rarely seen in Ireland at that time, and the tornister was particularly exotic looking.

These young men, who were about the same age as myself or younger, were members of the left-wing Young Prussian League. They came from Aachen or thereabouts, were strongly nationalist, and showed contempt for the terms of the Treaty of Versailles by carrying out military type reconnaissance exercises, unarmed, along and over the Belgian frontier in the area of Eupen and Malmédy, which they claimed were German-speaking and should still be part of Germany.

They had somehow established relations with Republican elements in the Irish Free State and had some knowledge of Irish history. As, next day, we entered the front gate of TCD, they asked was this the English or the Irish university. I said it was an Irish university established under the English régime in the sixteenth century. Having got over that hurdle, I was next asked what was the building on the right and why had it got the word NIKE over it. 'That is the new library building and it is a war memorial', I said. 'But NIKE means victory. What victory was that?' I was asked. I don't remember how I handled that one, but I dare say I voiced a strong objection to that use of the word NIKE, and the triumphalism suggested by it. My father would have done so. He felt that war memorials should celebrate peace, not victory.

The Young Prussians included Helmut Clissmann and Jupp Hoven. Clissmann subsequently married Elizabeth (Budge) Mulcahy, of a well-known Sligo Republican family who were close friends of Frank Ryan. Ryan, whom I met in the mid-thirties when I was working in the printing business at the Sign of the Three Candles, had taken the anti-Treaty side in the Irish civil war. He was a leading Left Republican personality and fought in the Spanish War (1936–39) as commander of the James Connolly Section of the International Brigade. With the defeat of the Republican forces, Ryan was condemned to death, but the sentence was not carried out and he was held in Burgos prison.

The Young Prussian League did not support the Nazi régime. It was regarded as *Nationalbolschevist,* but like all other organisations it was in due course *gleichgestaltet,* that is to say, forcibly absorbed into the Nazi network, though for a time its members were still regarded as politically unreliable.

Clissmann was head of the Academic Exchange Service in Ireland, with branches in Dublin, Cork and Galway. It was regarded by External Affairs as a front for espionage activities. On the outbreak of war, Clissmann was called up and returned to Germany. He and Hoven were accepted into the Abwehr, the Military Intelligence Service. This enabled Hoven to take the initial steps to have Frank Ryan released from Burgos prison and transferred to Germany. An attempt to land him in Ireland by submarine failed and he was allowed to live privately with the Clissmanns. He became ill and died in Dresden in 1944. Details of his story are given in, among other sources, *Geheimauftrag Irland* by Enno Stephan (1961), published later as *Spies in Ireland* (London, 1965), and in *Connolly Column* by Michael O'Riordan (Dublin, 1978).

The Clissmanns returned to Ireland after the war. Hoven, towards the end of his life, became a Free Democratic Party member of the Bundestag and died in 1971. An account of the war-time activities of Clissmann and Hoven, and also of Thomsen and Hempel, is given in *Neutral Ireland and the Third Reich* by John P. Duggan (1985) based on a detailed study of German Foreign Office papers.

When I look back at the academic year 1930–31 in Cambridge, German affairs continue to be my main interest. I was now treasurer of the Cambridge University Anglo-German Association, of which the Hon. Secretary was Hanns-Ulrich Kuester. In November 1930 he read a paper on 'The Development of National–Socialism in Germany', which was the first many of us had heard of this phenomenon. Kuester was from a village or small town near Trebnitz in Silesia, now incorporated in Poland, and he was half-Jewish; but he had no idea of the extent of the evil in the movement which he was describing. He subsequently acquired British citizenship and remained in England as a teacher, having changed his name to John Chester. He was my closest friend amongst the Germans at Cambridge and he stayed with us one time at Grianblah, where he was naturally, as Overbeck reminded me that he too had been, enraptured by Shamrock.

The high-light of the first years of the C. U. Anglo-German Association was the acceptance by the German Ambassador of our invitation to visit Cambridge. It was considered an important event and we gave a luncheon in his honour which was a great success. This was the first time that a German Ambassador had visited Cambridge officially since, I think, 1908. I conducted the ambassador and his wife on a tour of some of the colleges, and as a result of this personal contact I was invited to the embassy in London on the occasion of the visit of Reich Chancellor Brüning and Foreign Minister Curtius. The reception coincided with the Trooping of the Colour by the Brigade of Guards on the official birthday, in June, of King George V. This would be an occasion for formal dress, so I wrote home to Father to send me my school uniform — morning coat and striped trousers. I bought a top-hat from a pawnbroker for 3s.6d. and was so pleased with this purchase that I then bought a fawn waistcoat and white spats and gloves. This outfit, but without the spats, still occasionally appears at formal weddings and state funerals. Only the trousers have changed.

In the complete rig-out I took the train from Cambridge and walked the streets of London. The embassy was in Carlton House Terrace and had a great long terrace (in the other sense of the word) overlooking St James's Park and the Horse Guards Parade, so we had an excellent view of the colourful ceremony, while strolling about drinking champagne.

As to the two principal guests at the embassy, Heinrich Brüning was leader of the Catholic Centre Party in the Reichstag and Chancellor from 1930 to 1932 in a Germany seriously shaken by the world economic depression. He was the last significant statesman of the Weimar Republic, but his drastic austerity policies made him very unpopular and fostered extremism from right and left. His dismissal by the almost senile President von Hindenburg in 1932 cleared the way for the dictatorship which was to follow.

Julius Curtius was a Deutsche Volkspartei (rightist liberal) deputy. His presence in London in 1931 may well have had to do with what was to be his main achievement, namely his negotiation, together with Brüning, of a reduction in the burden of reparations, though these were still supposed to continue for sixty years.

The ambassador was Baron von Neurath, who was Minister for Foreign Affairs from 1932 to 1938 and, after the fall of Czechoslovakia, 'Reich Protector' for Bohemia and Moravia, but of such things we had no foreboding in 1931. In 1946 he was sentenced by International Military Tribunal to fifteen years imprisonment.

My time at Cambridge was coming to an end with the Easter Term of 1931. I loved Cambridge and greatly enjoyed my time there. but I was ready to move on to the next stage, whatever that was to be, and above all I wanted to get back to Ireland and make that my permanent base.

Because of the specialization which took place in English schools at secondary level, the normal degree course at English universities was three years, as against four years in the Irish universities. Another major difference was that final exams were held in Cambridge in the last week in May and results were out by mid-June. Students at Irish universities, whose exams were several months later, must have been at a distinct disadvantage in the competition for jobs for newly qualified graduates.

I passed Part II of the Modern and Medieval Languages Tripos with a Second Class, First Division, degree, with which I was well satisfied. Prof. Breul was very disappointed that I did not get a First; but Father had no doubt that I was not of First Class calibre and he told me that he would certainly not have given me a First Class degree.

I was not long home before I was required to put my knowledge of German to practical use.

My cousin, Gwendolen Bligh (later Barrington) was the principal breeder in Ireland of German Shepherd dogs, and continued to be so for over sixty years. In Ireland they were officially referred to by their correct name. In England they had to be called Alsatians, because they were introduced at about the time of World War I and it was not permissible to have anything German.

Gwen's father died on active service in 1915. Her mother died in 1928, and Gwen, an only child, inherited a considerable fortune, including Brittas, the property at Nobber, County Meath, where the family had been settled since 1641 or soon thereafter.

Gwen decided to finance the first ever German Shepherd Dog Show to be held in Ireland and to get a judge over from Germany. I was appointed interpreter for the show, should one be required. The judge, Herr Schertel, came from the Saarland and fortunately had a good Rhineland sense of humour. He was to arrive by the day mail from Holyhead and I was to meet him and look after him. At the last moment, word came that he was getting the night mail and would arrive at Dún Laoghaire early in the morning. For some reason, I was not free until 3 o'clock in the afternoon, nor was anyone else free for the day.

The secretary of the German Shepherd Dog Club was D.J. Smyth, of Dundrum, and he arranged to meet Schertel at Dún Laoghaire and put him on the train for Westland Row, where Smyth's brother would meet him. DJ phoned through to his brother that he would have no difficulty in spotting him as he was a small man in a green hat with a feather in it, and he had, said DJ, not a single word of English. The only German which the Smyths knew was the commands for dogs, which they needed because their dogs had come from Germany. The brother met Schertel at Westland Row, took him by the lead, so to speak, across the road to the Grosvenor Hotel, showed him into a bedroom, pointed to a bed, and said, '*Platz! da bleiben!* — lie down! stay there!' Then he pointed to three o'clock on his watch. Schertel related this to me, with great amusement, and said he had been dealing with dogs all his life, but this was the first time he had been spoken to like a dog.

The show was held at Clarke's Riding Academy, at Parkgate. The first class was assembled in a ring and Schertel and I stood in the centre. 'Are these supposed to be German Shepherd dogs?' he asked. 'What's he saying? What's he saying?' went up the cry, for the owners were very excited at having a German judge for the first time and wanted to know every word he said. 'They're ony fit for the slaughter-house', said Schertel, adding, 'You're not repeating that are you?' Indeed I wasn't, but I had to think of something to say.

He told me to tell them all to walk around the ring, and then to trot round it, and to keep trotting while we went off to judge the next class. This was unheard-of behaviour, but he said he wanted to see what condition they would be in after running for twenty minutes. One of the competitors in this class was Sir Valentine Grace, who was immensely portly. He was showing a bitch in pup and the longer he ran the more he looked as if he were going to pup himself. Fortunately he managed to send a signal to a kennel-man in a white coat who took over from him. I cannot remember what other devastating comments Schertel made or what difficulties I had in inventing a suitable substitute; but the show was, according to *Our Dogs* of 31 July 1931, voted a great success, though the green stars went to unknown dogs and former green star champions got nothing. There was an English judge for the obedience classes, and about thirty members of the club attended the dinner given in the Gresham Hotel for the two judges. At the dinner, I spoke on behalf of Schertel, who congratulated the breeders on having reached such a high standard, according to *Our Dogs.* That journal also carried my translation of the judge's report on the show as a whole and on each one of the one hundred and thirty dogs individually.

VII

Law and Economics

Before I came down from Cambridge I had already given up the idea of teaching as a career. I had got no encouragement from Father. I think he saw that I would not be happy in the parlous state, and on the very low pay, of the profession in Ireland at that time.So my thoughts turned to the civil service. I never shared the contempt for that profession which I was often to meet in later life. It seemed to me that there was a lot to be said for working for what one hoped was the common good, rather than for someone else's profit.

I realized that from the age of fifteen-and-a-half I had had a very specialized education and I decided to enlarge it, firstly by learning Irish and secondly by doing the two-year postgraduate course in the Law School of TCD leading to the degree of Bachelor in Laws. However, I went no further after passing the Intermediate Examination in Law in April 1932.

While attending lectures in TCD, I also attended the lectures of George O'Brien, Professor of Economics in University College Dublin. I used to go to a nine o'clock lecture in UCD, which was then in Earlsfort Terrace, and a ten o'clock lecture in TCD, or the other way round, getting from one to the other on my bike.

I was not enrolled in UCD and my attendance at these lectures was a private arrangement, thanks to an introduction from my brother-in-law, Diarmid Coffey. George O'Brien was the great authority on Irish economics and was a member of various commissions (agricultural, fiscal, economic, banking, derating) since 1922. He made friends with me, seventeen years his junior, and was very kind to me, often asking me out for walks and to dinner in one or other of the various clubs to which he belonged.

George was born in the heart of the city and lived in Dublin all his life, venturing hardly at all further than the strand at Portmarnock, where he was a member of the Golf Club. He was not happy at home in adult life. His father had died when he was fifteen years old and he was an only child. He lived the rest of his life with his mother, who had no understanding or appreciation of his achievements as a writer, journalist and lecturer.

James Meenan, his biographer, records that for some forty years he never spent an evening at home. He liked to get to know his students individually and the best of them he would invite out to dinner either alone with him or, if they were particularly promising, with some visitor from *The Economist* or *The Times.*

Among the interesting people I met in his company was Geoffrey Crowther, whom George had just then (1932) recommended to the Bank of Ireland as 'an adviser skilled in contemporary economic thinking' and who later became editor of *The Economist,* of which George was Dublin correspondent for twenty years from 1929.

Meenan was a younger man whom I met with George. He was a lecturer in political economy in UCD from 1936 and succeeded as Professor when George retired in 1961 after thirty-five years in the Chair. Like my father, George had never had any position in the university junior to that of professor. He died in 1973 at the age of eighty-one. Meenan's biography, *George O'Brien: A Biographical Memoir* (Gill & Macmillan, 1980), is based on George's own intimate journal.

Many of my dinners with George were in the Royal Irish Yacht Club, Dún Laoghaire. He had no interest in sailing, nor in most of the members of the club who, at the time he joined, were more Royal than Irish and frowned on him and the guests whom he entertained there. His nationalism was of a very moderate sort, akin to Dominion Home Rule, but he was on dining terms with many who were active in the public life of the Irish Free State and the Republic of Ireland.

In 1932, I was fortunate enough to be able also to attend Daniel Binchy's lectures. He had been Professor of Jurisprudence and Legal History in UCD from 1925. He was persuaded, reluctantly, to act as the first Irish Minister to Germany from 1929 to 1932, and was glad to take up his position in UCD again, after his return to Ireland, for the latter half of the academic year 1931-32. His lectures on International Law and Roman Law were a fascinating experience for me, as compared with the deadly dull lectures I was officially attending in TCD.

Douglas Gageby, reviewing in 1991 Andrée Sheehy-Skeffington's biography *Skeff: A Life of Owen Sheehy-Skeffington,* notes that in the thirties and forties academics (but definitely not 'Skeff') 'were known to read out of text-books to their students and to be indignant if the scholar did not slavishly take down verbatim notes.' That is somthing like what I was witnessing in TCD.

As against this, Binchy dealt with international law as one who had actually operated it officially and he dealt with Roman law by comparing and contrasting it all the time with Old Irish law, on which he was the leading authority.

My attending law and economics lectures was part of my preparation for an attempt to enter the Irish civil service, preferably External Affairs. I was interviewed for a cadetship in the Department of External Affairs and was quite rightly turned down, for my lack of general knowledge showed up very badly. George O'Brien, was on the interview board and I felt very sorry for him since he had declared his interest in me and therefore took no part in the interview and must have been very embarrassed at my poor performance.

My father was on friendly terms with H.F. Boland, Assistant Secretary, Department of Finance, who was one of the Civil Service Commissioners (and father of F.H. Boland, President of the UN General Assembly 1960–61), and Boland assured him that they would welcome a non-Roman Catholic in External Affairs. At the next intake of cadets one such was appointed, namely William

Warnock, or Liam Mac Giolla Mhearnóg (he was a very good Irish speaker). He was four years my junior and I knew him well. His first posting abroad was to Berlin, and there he found himself stuck as chargé d'affaires *ad interim* 1939–44. He was appointed ambassador to various places, including Switzerland and Canada, where I met him again in retirement on a couple of occasions and where he died in 1986.

I also tried for a post as Junior Administrative Officer, which I missed, but I was offered a position with the Revenue Commissioners which would have led to an Inspectorate of Taxes. This did not appeal to me, though the pay would eventually have been much more than I could expect in the job I was at, and after consultation with my then employer I rejected the offer, and thereby for ever closed the door on the civil service.

Once or twice when I was in and out of TCD, I joined my father's class for honours students when he invited me as he felt he was going to say something interesting. I told him afterwards that his lecture, which was given largely without reference to notes, was of a much higher intellectual standard than anything I had heard at Cambridge. I could see why his best students adored him, while others may have found him a bit difficult and some even regarded him as a figure of fun because of his eccentric manner.

VIII

Things Irish

My interest in law and economics was part of my programme for the enlargement of my education beyond the confines of the Modern and Medieval Languages Tripos. A much more long-term commitment was to the Irish language and other things Irish.

I started lessons with Mary Murphy, which I greatly enjoyed. Her husband, Gerard Murphy, was in a sanatorium in Switzerland. He recovered from TB and I met him when he returned to Ireland. From 1939 he was lecturer, and subsequently Professor of the History of Celtic Literature, in UCD and was well known as a writer on Irish literature of all periods.

Years before Gerard's return to Ireland, Mary had brought our lessons to an end and passed me on to Tomás Ó Ruairc, a lay teacher in a Christian Brothers school. I made good progress with him, both because I actually liked grammar and syntax and because I was determined to acquire a working knowledge of the language, and was enthusiastic about this.

Tomás wanted to interest me in another aspect of Gaelic culture by taking me to a hurley match. It was between University College Dublin and University College Cork. It was such a filthy game, with players attacking each other with their *camáin* in places on the field far removed from the ball, that I never wanted to see the game again. Nor did I until, when Bea was National President of the Irish Countrywomen's Association (1974–76), we were invited to the all-Ireland Final in Croke Park and seated with the VIPs. We then saw hurley at its best and it was as enjoyable to watch as a ballet.

Another step in my Gaelicization process was to learn Irish dancing. I made the acquaintance of a teenage schoolboy named George Leonard, who had won every possible award and medal for Irish dancing except one. To be defeated for that one award caused him great depression and to cheer him up I suggested that he might start teaching. Sheela and I were his first pupils. Sheela did not stick it as long as I did — she was also learning to play the Irish harp at that time — and my ultimate achievement was to dance an Irish hornpipe solo on the stage in Amsterdam, accompanied by Colm O Lochlainn, when we were attending a 'Common-Room Evening' — an assembly of Dutch youth — on the occasion of the first International Youth Hostel Conference in 1932. Mine was not a good performance, but the Dutch had never seen anything like it before.

George Leonard went on to become one of the best known of Irish dance instructors and adjudicators at *feiseanna.* He met a sudden death in the 1980s during a period of some very nasty 'gay-bashing' incidents on the north side of Dublin city.

A propos of my earlier efforts to read Irish at Cambridge, I mentioned my meeting with George Thomson. There are several references to him in *The Blaskets: A Kerry Island Library* by Muiris Mac Conghail (Country House, Dublin, 1987). George, like me, had wanted to read Irish (or Celtic languages) for his degree at Cambridge, but had to accept that the university did not offer an undergraduate course in that subject. Accordingly, he read classics and became a distinguished Greek and Homeric scholar. He was a Fellow of King's College, Cambridge, from 1927 to 1933 and taught for a time at TCD. He had learnt some modern Irish and became a regular visitor to the Blaskets from 1923, when he was twenty years old.

In 1931 he was appointed Lecturer in Ancient Classics through the medium of Irish in University College Galway. Mac Conghail has a good story of Thomson, a layman (classics lecturers were expected to be clerics) and an Englishman, from Cambridge University, astonishing the interview board with a lecture on Plato in Blasket Irish.

Thomson's close companion, of his own age, on the island was Muiris Ó Súilleabháin. Thomson persuaded him, firstly, to join the Gárda Síochána and, secondly, to write his autobiography, which appeared in 1933 as *Fiche Blian ag Fás,* subvented financially by Thomson, who could not accept the conditions laid down by An Gúm, the government publishing agency. The book was an instant success and Thomson set to work on its translation into English. This was to be the first translation into English of a genuine account of the life of the Irish peasant as written by one of themselves. Thomson, being English himself, was not capable of reproducing the Irish dialect of English without assistance, and this assistance came from Moya Llewelyn Davies. The translation, published in Dublin and London in 1933 as *Twenty Years A-Growing,* was an even greater success than the original.

Thomson was passionately interested in the language and literature of the islanders, their legends and folklore and the whole way of life on the islands, and he drew comparisons between that civilization and the civilization of ancient Greece.

While in Galway, he published four books in Irish on aspects of Greek scholarship. He devised a scheme of extension lectures to bring university learning into the villages and houses of the Gaeltacht, but the college was not interested and he left and returned to his Fellowship of King's College for another two years before becoming Professor of Greek at the University of Birmingham (1937–70) and writing many books, translated into twenty-two languages.

He was, or became, a Marxist and a member of the Communist Party of Great Britain and his books included *Marxism in Poetry, From Marx to Mao Tse-Tung* and *Capitalism and After,* as well as an important essay on *The Blasket That Was* (1982), published first in Irish as *An Blascaod Mar a Bhí* (1977), in which he draws comparisons with *Ancient Greek Society,* another of his titles.

Moya Llewelyn Davies had no profound knowledge of Irish;

but having been brought up by her grandparents in Kerry, her four sisters and her mother having all died in 1890 from eating contaminated shellfish, she was able to help George Thomson in rendering *Twenty Years A-Growing* into the appropriate Irish dialect of English.

Thomson introduced me to Moya, who lived in great comfort and elegance in Furry Park, a very fine 1730 house near Raheny, in north County Dublin, which her husband, Crompton Llewelyn Davies, had bought in 1920. I never met Crompton, whom Moya always spoke of with affection, but he lived in London and I don't think he ever came to Ireland during my time. He was interested in social and political affairs, in economics and land reform and in the Liberal Party and he had become a close friend of Lloyd George and was appointed Solicitor General to the British Post Office, a position which he lost in 1921 on account of his strong support of Moya's Irish nationalist activities. He was perhaps the only civil servant not an Irishman to have lost his job for supporting Irish nationalism. His close friends, whom Moya helped to entertain when they were living in London, included Bertrand Russell and Sir James Barrie, whose Peter Pan stories were based on the family of Crompton's brother.

Crompton and Moya were in touch with leaders of the Irish nationalist movement, especially Michael Collins, for whom Furry Park became a refuge during the Anglo-Irish War and during the negotiations on the Treaty, on the drafting of which Crompton gave advice to Collins. Some of the above information comes from the booklet produced in 1985 by the Furry Park Action Group, which was set up to oppose a plan for the demolition of the house and succeeded in preventing this. When I was in touch with the author and told him of my frequent visits to that house and of my youthful interest in Michael Collins, he asked me if I had ever heard it suggested that there were sexual relations between Moya and Michael. I had never heard this suggestion previously, but I said that she had told me herself that they were lovers. I had never before mentioned this to anyone. I did however know that some people who were old enough to have known what was going on in the early 1920s, expressed their disapproval of Moya. That affair may have been the reason or it may simply have been because she was living apart from her husband, though amply provided for by him. Only when Tim Pat Coogan's biography, *Michael Collins,* was published (Hutchinson, 1990) did I learn that it had been freely rumoured that Collins and Moya became lovers, and that she openly claimed this to be the case.

Moya liked giving small elegant dinners, with champagne, sometimes alone with me, and I would stay for the night. Sometimes there were other visitors present and I had the excitement of meeting some of the leaders in the struggle for independence and founders of the Irish Free State. One of these was Desmond FitzGerald, revolutionary and statesman, playwright and philosopher. Born and brought up in England, he had lived for some years in France before coming to Ireland in 1913. He had fought in the GPO in the Easter Rising of 1916, had been in and out of jail, and had edited Dáil Éireann's underground sheet, *The Bulletin*. On the establishment of the Irish Free State he became Minister for External Affairs, and when I met him, he was Minister for Defence.

Another dinner guest was Ernest Blythe (or Earnán de Blaghd), Minister for Finance, Irish language enthusiast, and theatre manager, the only Northern Protestant to become a cabinet minister in the South. He had been active in the Irish Volunteers and had been arrested and imprisoned many times.

Then there was James MacNeill, another Northerner, who had retired from a successful career in the Indian civil service to join the Sinn Féin movement and was Governor-General of the Irish Free State from 1928 to 1932. He would have been accompanied at the dinner by his wife, Josephine. Later, as a widow, she was in 1949 appointed by Seán MacBride as the first Irish ambassador to the Netherlands. She was the first Irish woman to achieve diplomatic status and she continued to serve as an ambassador until her retirement in 1960. I met her on many occasions, mainly because of Bea's connection with the Irish Countrywomen's Association, of which Josephine was a distinguished member and one of their first batch of Buan-Cháirde, or Honorary Life Members.

It would be difficult to imagine now, when our cabinet ministers are so readily accessible, what a thrill it was for me in those early days, as I was just settling into Irish life, to meet such statesmen and ex-revolutionaries as FitzGerald and Blythe, and sometimes to be driven away with them from Furry Park in their very unpretentious black Ford cars, made in Cork, squeezed in beside their armed detectives.

Moya had two children, Richard, born 1912, and Katherine, who was always called Seán and dressed in boy's clothes when this was not at all the done thing. Richard became an architect and shared with his friend, William Griffith, an office at the top of the building which housed the Unicorn Restaurant in Merrion Row. Neither of them practised much as architects in Ireland. Richard went to England, where he became consultant to *The Times* and the Stock Exchange, Professor of Architecture in University College, London, 1960–69, and Professor of Urban Planning from 1969. In recognition of his work in urban planning he was made a Life Peer in 1963, as Baron Llewelyn-Davies. He died in 1981. Remarkably, his wife, Patricia, another architect (with LMS Railways 1942–48), whom he married in 1943, was also in 1967 created a Life Peer, as Baroness Llewelyn-Davies of Hastoe. That must surely be something of a record, for husband and wife to be sitting in the House of Lords at the same time.

My introduction to Moya arose out of my interest in the Irish language. In further efforts to cultivate my knowledge of the language I went to the Aran Islands, off the coast of Galway, in the summer of 1932. I spent six weeks on Inis Meáin, the middle one of the three islands and the most inaccessible.

The steamer went out from Galway twice a week and took about four hours to get to the islands, but it was only at Inis Mór (the Big Island) that it could sail into harbour. At the other islands it stood off and anchored out to sea, and passengers, goods and mail bags were offloaded into currachs. With the steamer rolling, as it always did, and the currachs bobbing up and down, though handled with superb skill, this was, to say the least of it, an exciting experience.

I was allotted accommodation with the family of Patch Bhrianín, i.e. Patrick, son of little Brian. As so many on the island had the same surname, e.g. Conghaile (anglicized Conneely), it was largely dispensed with. I was well received by Patch and his immensely tall and stately wife — so unusual that whenever I said I was staying with Patch Bhrianín I always got the reply, *'nach íontach mór an bhean atá aige!* — hasn't he the wonderful big wife!'

They had only one child, a babe in arms. Some thirty years later I was driving towards the quays in Galway when I saw a young woman carrying her bags, evidently on the way to the boat. She accepted a lift in my car and turned out to be that babe in arms of Patch Bhrianín. Her parents had fed me well (except when the delicious lamb, roasted in the pot hanging over the turf fire, turned out to be magotty) always in my own room, which seemed to be the accepted practice. I found it exceedingly difficult to make contact with them. They had no English; in any case we used no English on the island — except with the nurse when I needed medical attention after the magotty lamb! I suppose I simply failed to bridge the culture gap and did not, for instance, say the Rosary with them. I did not at the time know the words in English, let alone Irish. Nevertheless I was fascinated with everything about the islanders and I wrote about them in somewhat romantic terms in an article which appeared in the October 1933 issue of *The Hiker and Camper,* a monthly magazine of whch I was Irish Editor in 1933, having contributed to it regularly in 1932, mostly notes on An Óige, the Irish Youth Hostel Association. I think I was paid a few shillings, but my main reward was the solid brass torch, made for Welsh miners, which I still always carry with me if I walk out on a dark night.

On Inis Meáin I spent most of my time with the other *stróinséirí,* visitors who had come to practice their Irish. The two who attracted me most turned out to be Protestant national school teachers. So ignorant was I, that I did not know that there was such a thing as a Protestant national school. There was an understanding amongst the *stróinséirí* that we did not speak any English together, unless one was at a loss for a word. When I found that I could carry on a flirtation through the medium of Irish, I felt that I was really making progress with the language!

One of the teachers was Márta Ní Ríada, from Dublin. I lost touch with her soon after returning to the mainland and I had not seen her for some forty years when one day I was dining with Bea in Restaurant na Mara, in Dún Laoghaire, and Márta came up and identified herself. She had Alec Reid with her, whom she described as her favourite uncle. He was, or had been, a TCD lecturer with a particular interest in Samuel Beckett, and it was to him that Bea had given her reminiscence which is quoted by Deirdre Bair in her biography, *Samuel Beckett* (Picador edition, 1980, pp. 25–26). The story is that the Orpen family sat in a pew facing the Becketts' in Tullow Church, Carrickmines, and that Bea remembered Sam frowning at her week after week during services, and years later discovered that 'his dissatsifaction was nothing personal — it was towards the whole cosmos rather than with me in particular'.

When Bea and I were married and were living in the upper half of a two-storey Georgian house at 73 Terenure Road East, I offered the use of a room in the house for weekly lessons in Irish, specifically for adults with no knowledge of the language. This was a service provided by Craobh na hAiséirí (The Branch of the Resurgence), a branch of Conradh na Gaeilge (the Gaelic League). The class consisted entirely of men and women who had been either to school in England or to one of the few schools in Ireland where no Irish was taught. It included, for a time, John Betjeman, UK press attaché, later to become Poet Laureate.'Ireland's favourite spy', John P. Duggan calls him. The classes came to an end when I left Dublin in 1942. I never felt that they had been a great success, for the teacher liked to address the class in Irish and found it impossible to grasp that there were well educated adults, Irish men and women, living in Ireland, who had not, and did not understand, a single word of Irish, and that the *modh díreach,* the direct method, might be the right thing for children, but was not suitable for the adult mind. However, the effect of the classes stayed on, for I have a postcard from Betjeman, dated 8 July 1943, addressed to me in Drogheda in Irish and written almost entirely in Irish.

Apart from the language another aspect of national culture in which I was actively interested was, as I have already mentioned, Irish dancing. I almost never went, or wanted to go, to 'foreign' dances, but I often went to céilithe (or céilís), for which I sometimes donned my green kilt or, later, my MacKenzie tartan kilt. I also sometimes wore one or other kilt on public occasions other than céilithe. The MacKenzie dress tartan is one of the prettiest of all and I was happy to be able to claim a right to it by virtue of my mother's grandmother being a MacKenzie, with a traceable descent from the original Kenneth, founder of the clan, who died in 1304, and with some claims to a pedigree stretching back a further twelve generations into the mists of the Highland Celts.

At some quite informal céilí, frequented by UCD students, I met Karen, who was Swedish. She was interested in my weekend pastime of hill walking, but had never done any in Ireland. I was going off the following weekend with Ronald Brown and a German friend of his, Heinrich Petri. Karen came with us. We took the train to Glenealy, walked through the woodlands, and spent the night at Kilmacurra House, an elegant country house which had just been opened as a high-class guest-house, one of the first of its kind, run by a German named Budina. It had a splendid arboretum, one of the finest collections of trees in Ireland. It is now national property.

Karen and I went away together many times after that. We were walking through Powerscourt Demesne one day, when we met Viscount Powerscourt, whom I knew slightly, raking leaves along the avenue and burning them. He was Chief Scout of the Boy Scouts of Ireland, who had permanent camping sites on his demesne, and he had agreed to my request to include his name on the first list of Patrons of An Óige in 1931. So I stopped to speak to him and told him that my friend was from Sweden. He invited us to call into the house as we were passing, and he went on ahead in his little car. We walked on and when we reached the house he had the Swedish flag flying from the flag-pole on the front lawn. Karen was delighted!

On another occasion we found ourselves at Brittas Bay, County Wicklow, on a fine day with a high tide. There was nobody on the beach, nor in the sand-dunes as far as we could see. Either because we had no bathing togs with us or because we did not want to be bothered with them, we went swimming without them. I did not know that I was being spied on by somebody who had, as it turned out, taken a fancy to me and in whom I had never expressed any interest. She reported my misbehaviour to my good friend, Thekla Beere, who told me that she did not care what I did in my private life, but that as National Secretrary of An Óige my behaviour was highly reprehensible and could cause serious damage to the good name of the Association, then in its infancy. She was quite right and I was more circumspect from then on.

Karen was secretary to the Swedish Consul-General and in due course I was invited to a cocktail party in the consulate in Fitzwilliam Square. I knew no one at the party, but I chatted with two smartly dressed women, who were standing alone, and one of them, Aileen, invited me to dinner at her house. I said that there were two of me, that the consul's secretary was my friend, and Aileen said to bring her along too and that we would drive out there with her husband, Brinny. So the four of us got into his Delage, which was coloured black and gold — his racing colours, as I learnt later. We drove at 120 mph through Phoenix Park and for a few miles out into the country, through the gates of a magnificent demesne and up to a splendid nineteenth-century castellated mansion. I do not know whether Karen knew whom we were with, but I certainly did not.

There were other guests already in residence and Brinny spread the word that the men were not to dress for dinner (to their obvious displeasure) because he had brought one guest who had not got his dinner-jacket with him. We sat down ten to dinner in a splendid vaulted dining-room (it now has a false ceiling), waited on by footmen. Aileen sat me on her left and amused herself because she knew that I did not know who she was, and that I suddenly discovered, from something she said, that she must be a Guinness. She was in fact a daughter of the Hon. Ernest Guinness, son of the 1st Viscount Iveagh, and was married to her second cousin, the Hon. Brinsley Plunket, son of the 5th Baron Plunket.

Brinny was a long way off at the other end of the dinner-table and Karen, with whom he was no doubt entranced, was on his right. When the ladies withdrew and we sat around the port he said to me, 'I understand that you are not interested in horses. Then, what are you interested in?' — a difficult question to answer in a company whose sole interest was horses.

We joined the ladies for a very racy game of charades and in the early hours of the morning the only other non-resident guests, leaving in their car, were asked to drive Karen and me back to Fitzwilliam Square. Our driver, whose name was Cairnes, and who was wearing the dress uniform of the Egyptian police, was, as soon became apparent, in no fit state to drive at all. On that narrow winding road, leading past Castleknock College to the Phoenix Park (White's Gate), he bounced from one side of the road to the other and as we approached the Park we saw that the gates were closed. 'I hope he hits them in the middle', I said, 'otherwise we are done for'. Hit them in the middle he did, with an almighty bang, which caused lights to appear in the gate-lodge. The gates were barred, bolted, chained and locked, but we drove through them to the other side. Cairnes got out, straightened the bashed front wings and drove on and we eventually got to Fitzwilliam Square.

Some fifteen years later, Bea and I were lunching at Stameen, the residence of Colonel Cairnes, outside Drogheda. (It is now the Boyne Valley Hotel.) Bea was on Col. Cairnes's right and I was one place further down on his left. I picked up eye signals from Bea and saw that she was smiling broadly because Col. Cairnes was embarking on The Story of the Man Who Drove through the Closed Gates of the Phoenix Park. When I told him that I was in the car and, briefly, how I came to be there, he said, 'But they were not your sort of people!' — which indeed they were not. Cairnes of the Egyptian police, it turned out, was a nephew of the colonel's.

My sort of people or not, Aileen asked me to come back and stay the next weekend and help to guide people through the house, which was being opened to the public in aid of the Jubilee Nurses. The house was Luttrellstown Castle, built about 1800 and incorporating portions of a medieval castle. In the last century it was considered one of the principal show places in the neighbourhood of Dublin, mainly because of its well landscaped demesne, complete with lake, Doric temple, a series of waterfalls and a Gothick ruin, and it was visited by many of the writers of tours of Ireland during that period. I did my homework by studying the chapter on Luttrellstown in F.E. Ball's *History of the County of Dublin, Part IV*, and the history of the Guinness and Plunket families whose portraits adorned the walls. Hundreds of people came to view the place on that sunny summer afternoon and I was amused to see Aileen attach herself to one of my groups, to see what she could learn from me about her own house.

I met Aileen again at Luggala, in the Wicklow Mountains. It had been her father's property and he had left it, much to Aileen's chagrin, to his youngest daughter, Oonagh, whose second husband was the 4th Baron Oranmore and Browne. Hence Luggala descended to its present owner, Garech Onórach de Brún. Brinny died on active service in 1941. Aileen married secondly and lived in America for some years, returning to Luttrellstown in her advanced years, and I dined with her there over half a century after the first occasion and just shortly before the place was finally sold and its contents dispersed.

It was through Karen that I met Aileen. In another episode with Karen, she said to me one evening, 'The Childers are having a bottle party. Let's go!' So we got our two bottles of wine and arrived at 68 Highfield Road, Rathgar. The door was opened by Ruth, Erskine's wife, and my introduction of myself to her was something like, 'My father is a great admirer of your husband's grandmother'. That was a reference to Margaret Cushing Osgood, compiler of the most interesting and remarkable anthology I have ever come across, namely, *The City Without Walls: An Anthology setting forth the Drama of Human Life* (764pp, London, 1932). It consists of passages of prose and verse from all the great European and Oriental literatures, ancient and modern, some given in the original Latin, Italian, French, German, Welsh or Irish, with or without translation. My copy bears Mrs Osgood's autograph dated 1934. She lived with her daughter, Molly Childers, Erskine's mother, in Bushy Park Road, quite close to Highfield Road.

I had met Erskine once before when he was advertising manager of *The Irish Press* and he arranged to give An Óige a full page spread as an advertising feature. It appeared on 7 April 1933. Erskine and I had just failed to overlap at Cambridge, he coming down in 1928 as I was going up. He then went to Paris for four years as European manager of a very exclusive American travel organization and returned to Ireland when the first Fianna Fáil government came into power, as the result of the General Election of February 1932.

That was the first election at which I was entitled to vote, and I voted for Fianna Fáil. Andrée Sheehy-Skeffington, writing of that time in *Skeff: A Life of Owen Sheehy-Skeffington*, says of her husband: 'Owen was hoping for important gains by Fianna Fáil. De Valera's programme seemed to offer a more acceptable social policy, less repressive measures and a better chance of internal peace'. Shortly after the election, de Valera went to the League of Nations and made a speech 'which Owen admired and was often to quote as an example of de Valera's early social programme, clear-sighted and close to socialism, and his unfulfilled promise'.

I quote these sentences, because they reminded me, better than I could recall for myself, what my feelings were at the time. I continued to vote for Fianna Fáil until they lost their radical image and became as conservative as Cumann na nGaedheal, or Fine Gael as they came to be called. I even voted for Fianna Fáil in 1937, while voting against de Valera's constitution, *Bunreacht na hÉireann.*

I objected to the name of Éire being applied to the Twenty-six Counties, which I saw would happen, to the prohibition on laws providing for the dissolution of marriage, to the non-recognition of such dissolution granted under the law of another state and to the reference to the right to exercise jurisdiction over the whole of the national territory and to the special position of the Roman Catholic church. These features shattered my hopes for a pluralist society and a united Ireland.

Palmerston Park, where I lived with my father, was only a few minutes walk from Highfield Road, where the Childers lived and I was a frequent visitor to their house. There I was to meet many of the intelligentsia of Dublin, as well as some of the leaders of Fianna Fáil, up to and including Éamon de Valera.

IX

Three Candles

Trí caindle forosnat cach ndorcha:
Fír–Aicned–Ecna
Three candles that light up every darkness:
Truth–Nature–Knowledge

FROM THE *TRIADS OF IRELAND*

One of my father's interests was good typography and book production. An early example of his interest was a book he had privately printed in 1903. It was the autobiography of Thomas Cooke-Trench, who died in November 1902, leaving an account of his life in manuscript. My father had it printed at the Printinghouse, Galway, and bound by A.Thom & Co., Dublin. With its wide margins and half-binding in vellum, it was in a style of its time, but showing a degree of elegance which was out of the ordinary.

In 1930, after my mother's death, Father again wanted to produce something very much out of the ordinary, namely his *Contacts with Reality*, consisting of an elegiac essay and a critical note. For this he went to Colm O Lochlainn, who had a printing and publishing business, At the Sign of the Three Candles, in Fleet Street, Dublin.

He and Colm got on well together and, arising out of this transaction, I went to see Colm. I was twenty-two years old and still uncertain of what I should do. Colm took me onto his staff and there I remained for just short of ten years. My first job was proof-reading, my pay being £1 a week.

The particular work on which I started was Colm's new edition of (Sir) William Wilde's *Lough Corrib*. Colm had by chance discovered, some years previously, twenty of the original woodblocks which had been cut to illustrate the book, first published in 1867. This inspired Colm to reprint the original text.

In one respect he made, as he says in the Preface, drastic changes, namely in the spelling and elucidation of place-names. He explains that in many instances the spelling in the first edition agrees neither with the Ordnance Survey map nor with the original Gaelic version. He tried to give an intelligent Irish rendering of each name, but unfortunately he often changed his mind about what that rendering should be. And when I was compiling the index, I had to list a number of variants of each name, including the Ordnance Survey spelling for those readers who could not follow the Gaelic.

The book was not published until 1936. Its production was spread over a number of years. It was one of those jobs that were always on stand-by; they were not required by any particular date, and a few sheets would be printed off now and then whenever the appropriate machine was standing idle. In spite of this it is a respectable specimen of book production, apart from the inconsistency in the spellings.

In the Preface, Colm gives voice to one of his pet grievances — 'the mutilation of our place-names by the map-makers of the [Ordnance] Survey. Why, for example, must we be content with ILLAUNAGEERAGH while our Scottish brothers have EILEAN NAN CAORACH? Why have all our lakes become Lough while in Scotland they remain Loch?' And so on. I share Colm's view, and since those days I have always used the form Loch in such names as Glendaloch, for instance. That is my mild protest against what Colm calls 'the mischief wrought by the name-coiners of the Survey'. I think that Colm must have realized that his much more drastic protest was a mistake and that he had in fact made confusion worse confounded, which he had prayed not to do, for he made no similar attempt to rectify place-names when he reprinted, in 1949, Wilde's *The Beauties of the Boyne and the Blackwater*, again adorned with the original woodcuts as first published in 1849.

I started at the Three Candles as Colm's personal secretary, but soon became the company's secretary and accountant, and eventually general manager, at £7 per week. Colm was the leading Irish authority and practitioner in typography and print-design. Any job going through the plant in which he took a personal interest was sure to be of a high standard, and even in the general run of commercial work, which was the company's 'bread and butter', we had the reputation of being the best printers in Dublin, both in letterpress and in offset lithography, and amongst the best bookbinders too.

Colm was on excellent terms with all his employees, of whom there were about fifty, and with their respective trade unions. He was more concerned that they should have a decent living (their union rates were among the highest in Dublin) than that the business should make a big profit. Colm and his fellow-director, Andrew Devereux, drew little out of it, and he depended for a steady income on lecturing to the librarianship students in UCD and the printing trade apprentices in Bolton Street Technical School, home of the Dublin School of Printing and Book Production, of which he was part-time director from 1929.

In his approach to capital and labour, Colm O Lochlainn accepted much of the principles of the papal encyclical of 1891, *Rerum novarum*, which laid down Catholic teaching on the duty of society to the worker and the duty of the worker to society. Rev. A.W. Hutton says that this encyclical 'was slightly tinged with modern Socialism; it was described as "the social Magna Carta of Catholicism", and it won for Leo XIII the name of "the working-man's Pope"' (*Encyclopaedia Britannica*, 11th edition, xvi, 438). It came to the fore again about the time I joined Colm, since it was adapted and revised in 1931 in Pius XI's encyclical, *Quadragesimo anno*. Perhaps I may add that the Dublin master printers were largely people who would not pay heed to papal encyclicals and who, having no such guiding principles, appeared to act solely on the basis of profit-making — or so it seemed to me from the few contacts I had with them.

I carried some of Colm's philosophy with me in later life when I moved to Drogheda and found myself in charge of a business, owned by a strongly Protestant family, in which a standard piece of stationery was a printed form which read, 'Due to an industrial dispute, these premises will be closed until further notice', or words to that effect. The first time a dispute seemed likely to arise and I expressed my support for the workers, a special meeting of the three directors was called — the chairman/managing director, his brother and the widow of another brother. I was asked to state my views and then to leave the meeting. The directors heard for the first time a suggestion that there were other things to be considered besides profits, which were considerable. I won the day and for the twenty-two-and-a-half years I was there we never had an industrial dispute, or at least none of any consequence. When I tendered my resignation in 1965 and the word spread that I was leaving, one of the charge hands, expressing his regret, asked me if I would like him to organize a strike to protest against my departure!

I could not have undertaken my work on the *Loch Corrib* reprint without the knowledge I had of the Irish language, however limited. My cultural development in this regard was greatly enhanced by working with Colm. He was a Celtic scholar, with a good knowledge of Scottish Gaelic, as well as a profound knowledge of Irish, and a particular interest in Irish traditional music and songs. Benedict Kiely recalls that Colm used to give immensely entertaining lectures in Irish, dragging in all sorts of subjects, to the students of Celtic literature in UCD.

Many Irish speakers came to see Colm in Fleet Street about one thing or another and I regularly heard Irish spoken as a normal means of communication.

In 1931 Colm and Fionán Mac Coluim founded An Claisceadal, a group of people who were deeply concerned to rescue, and to hand on to the rising generation, songs in which Irish-speaking people had celebrated their day-to-day human experiences. They met at weekly winter sessions during the next ten years or so and were successful in planting the songs like seeds in the public mind, thus ensuring their survival. Some of the songs they 'discovered' became known to, and sung by, schoolchildren throughout Ireland. Colm introduced me to these sessions, whose characteristic was the fun and cheerfulness of the singing, but they were held on Saturday afternoons, when I wanted to be away walking in the Wicklow mountains, and I did not keep up my attendance.

However, I had the interest and pleasure of meeting those who were engaged in writing down the melodies, at the dictation of Colm or Fionán, which we then printed and published at the Three Candles, first in tonic sol-fa and later in staff notation. The first of these music writers, and official accompanist to An Claisceadal, was Michael Bowles, a cadet in the Army School of Music, who went on to become director of music, Radio Éireann. He established the RÉ Symphony Orchestra and founded in 1942 the RÉ public symphony concerts, which were successful beyond all expectations. There was disagreement on the rapidity with which thirty-five unemployed musicians from the Continent were taken on, thus upsetting the balance of the orchestra as he saw it, but the exact causes of his resignation from RÉ have always been something of a mystery. Leaving Ireland, he became principal conductor of the New Zealand Symphony Orchestra, and he worked in the USA and England and conducted in Brussels and Rome. On his retirement, he came home and embarked on the publication of more of the Irish songs from the eighteenth and nineteeth centuries which Colm, Fionán and others had collected. He gave them accompaniments and English translations. At the launch of the first volume, in 1985, he was kind enough to remember me 'from a thousand years ago!' as one of the few people surviving who could recall the earliest days of An Claisceadal, and the only one who could produce from his pocket, at the launch, the complete set of Claisceadal leaflets from the 1930s and 1940s. They were foolscap octavo (pocket size).

Another person who had to do with the early Claisceadal publications was Séamus Ennis. Séamus's father, Jimmy, was a well-known piper. Colm used to go out to him in the village of Finglas every Thursday evening, to teach him Irish in exchange for lessons on the uileann pipes. He took me with him on one occasion. Séamus was in his mid-teens, just out of school — all his schooling was through the medium of Irish — and was awaiting the call into the Civil Service, when he happened to meet Colm in UCD and Colm offered him a job at the Three Candles.

Colm must have known that Séamus had a remarkable facility for writing clear staff notation. He set him to preparing the music for the printing of An Claisceadal, a task that took him four years. He then went to work for the Irish Folklore Commission, travelling up and down the west coast of Ireland on his bicycle, collecting traditional music and songs. Later he joined RTÉ and the BBC, collecting in Scotland as well as Ireland. He was the first to record Willie Clancy, musician and folklorist, and, next to him, became perhaps the best-known piper and traditional musician in Ireland.

Colm was friends with all the leading Irish folklorists and took me to the West on one of his folklore-collecting weekends. We stopped in Athenry to meet his old friend, the parish priest, Canon Conroy (who died worth £100, Michael Bowles told me — a mark in his favour!). They greeted each other most cordially and then Canon Conroy spotted me standing quietly in the background, and asked who I was. *'Mhuise'*, said Colm, *'is duine gallda é, de mhuintir Trinseach.' 'Trinseach?'* says the canon. 'Trench? Well there was a Dr Trench down here was a friend of Dean Swift and wherever they were staying together this night they fell into an argument and the argument had not ended before it was time to go to bed. When Dr Trench got up in the morning he found a note slipped under the door which said,

You'll find grace in the pulpit and wit on the bench,
But nothing but dirt will you find in a trench.

I was delighted with this piece of genuine folklore, handed down verbally for generations and now recorded for the first time, though I have told it on many occasions.

That night we stayed in Galway, on Taylor's Hill, close to my birthplace, in the house of Senator Liam Ó Buachalla, Professor of Economics (through the medium of Irish) at University College, Galway. There I met his wife, Máire Ní Scolaí, whom I much admired and who became, and remains, my favourite traditional Irish singer. We went on into Conamara, where among our principal contacts were Mícheál Ó Droighneáin at Furbo and Josie Mongan, TD and hotelier, at Carna. Mícheál was a national school teacher, with an impressive library of books in several European languages.

Colm had been in the nationalist movement and was the youngest member of the committee set up in October 1913 which resulted in the formation of the Irish Volunteers, of which Colm was a Captain in 1916. The chairman of that committee, and later Chief of Staff of the Volunteers, was Eóin Mac Neill, from County Antrim, Vice-President of the Gaelic League and Professor of Early Irish History at UCD. Colm was one of a party of five who were despatched by Michael Collins on Good Friday 1916 to Kerry to take delivery of a shipload of German arms. Three of the party were drowned when their car drove into the river. The German ship was intercepted and scuttled and the arms were never landed. Colm returned to Dublin and was then one of those who were despatched by MacNeill to countermand the orders of the secret IRB (Irish Republican Brotherhood) to mobilize the Volunteers for the Easter Rising. In the ensuing confusion and the split which followed, Colm remained faithful to MacNeill.

There was seldom any necessity for Colm to go down the country to see any of our printing business customers, but he did take me with him one time to visit the Cistercian monks at Mount St Joseph's Abbey, Roscrea, a unique experience for me. They had a secondary school for boys there, for whom we produced their annual, *Fiolar,* over a number of years, so Colm was well known to some of the Cistercian Fathers. We dined with the whole community in the total silence of the refectory. This was followed, in due course, by Compline, sung in plain chant, which was new to me and which I found very beautiful. They used the immense volumes which one associates with medieval monasteries. And so to bed, each to our little cell.

Another journey I made with Colm took place soon after his father, John O'Loughlin, died in 1933. He was a partner in the printing firm of O'Loughlin, Murphy and Boland, which became insolvent and was wound up. Mr O'Loughlin took it upon himself to pay off all the firm's debts. To do this, he sought employment elsewhere. When Colm set up in business in 1929, he employed his father as our principal representative throughout Ireland for the sale of ordinary commercial printing and stationery. He did pay off the debts, which he was not legally obliged to do. It was while he was on a journey for us in Galway, that we got word from his hotel that he had been taken ill. Colm drove down and phoned back to tell me that his father had died and I had to break the news by calling personally on Colm's two married sisters.

Colm was shaken by his father's passing and some weeks later was glad to get away from everything by coming with me to the second International Youth Hostel Conference, in Bad Godesberg, Germany, where Chamberlain and Hitler were to meet five years later. We went by a HAPAG transatlantic liner from Cobh to Hamburg and on by train. After the conference, we visited some of the leading typographers, print designers and type founders in Frankfurt-am-Main, such as Rudolf Koch and Fritz Kredel, to whom Colm was already known, and from whom I acquired their beautifully designed volumes of Christian symbols and humorously illustrated German soldiers' songs.

Another German connection we had was that when I joined the Three Candles, the junior lithographic artist had just returned from Leipzig, to which Colm had sent him for training. Leipzig was the European centre of printing and bookselling, but it was unusual for anyone from Ireland to train there. Admittedly, our trainee, Karl Uhlemann, born and reared in Dublin, was of German parentage, his father being a chef in the Gresham Hotel, Dublin. Karl became well known as a draughtsman and designer, and his son, Raimund, followed in his footsteps as a designer for Aer Lingus.

The printing of books in Irish, in what was known as Gaelic script, presented difficulties to anyone with a sense of typographical design. For instance, there were no designed capital letters. So we simply used a larger size of lower-case letters. And there were no modern typefaces and no display types. Colm was the first to introduce the Hammerschrift from Germany, with specially designed accented letters. It was a beautiful display type and became very popular. We are talking about individual metal characters for setting by hand. As to mechanical setting, it was the hot-metal era and Colm strongly favoured the Monotype, which cast the letters as individual pieces of metal, rather than the solid line of the Linotype.

Colm designed a special fount, which was produced by Monotype and was appropriately called Colum Cille. It had properly designed capitals, lower-case, accented letters and the complete Roman alphabet. In the Gaelic alphabet there is no j k q v w x y or z. Technically, and artistically, it was a great success, though not a commercial success for Monotype. Besides the Three Candles there were few other printers who made use of it.

It was because of Colm's position as Ireland's leading typographer that I proposed him, my fellow-delegate at the first International Youth Hostel Conference in 1932 and again in 1933, as one of a sub-committee of three whose job it was to produce an international sign language for use in youth hostel handbooks. Switzerland produced the designs and Colm negotiated with the Monotype Corporation which produced the matrices. The result is the signs which are familiar to youth hostellers throughout the world.

Our printing inks at the Three Candles mostly came from Leipzig. Soon after I started in the business, Hans Zülch, the son of one of our principal suppliers, came over to see how the business was run and to improve his English. He stayed in my family home for some months. He had done the same in Spain and was looking forward to repeating the exercise in China, these countries being amongst his principal markets. He was a charming young man, in his early twenties, good-looking and highly cultured, interested in poetry and the fine arts, and very good company.

I visited him in Leipzig in 1935, on my way back from the fourth International Youth Hostel Conference in Poland, and I was startled to see him on the station platform in the black uniform of an SS officer. That was at a time when it was as acceptable to be an officer in the SS as to be an officer in a British Guards regiment. Hans wrote to me once or twice when he was on active service during the war. He had been through the Polish campaign and was caught up in the euphoria of German victory. I eventually heard from his agent in Dublin that he had been killed on the Eastern Front.

When Colm and I visited Frankfurt in 1933, one of our business contacts drove us up to Schardau and we stayed a couple of days with Aunt Zinnie. Colm was very charming and greatly enjoyed the visit. That was the year before Aunt Zinnie died.

Aunt Zinnie was not wholeheartedly opposed to the Nazi régime. She commented favourably to me on, for instance, the appearance of the Volunteer Labour Corps, tramping past the gate of Schardau. She knew of the six million unemployed and the hundreds of suicides in the economic chaos and despair of the last days of the Weimar Republic, and like many millions of others in Germany she saw some hope in the new régime's policy to tackle unemployment and to free Germany from some of the iniquities of the Versailles Diktat. She did not live to see how evil the Nazi régime became.

She did, however, object to the Swastika flag being hoisted in the direct line of her view from Schardau, when the Nazis built an *Erholungsheim*, or recreation centre, at Falkenstein. She protested so vigorously that the flag was actually moved out of her sight. Soon after that date that would have been a very dangerous protest to make, with unspeakable consequences for the protester.

Aunt Zinnie died on 17 December 1934 and my father and I were anxious to get out to Germany as quickly as possible for the obsequies. We decided to fly and we flew first to London from the military airfield at Baldonnel. Aer Lingus did not come into existence until 1936 and I have been unable to find any record of regular scheduled services before that. Pearse Cahill, of Iona National Airways, tells me that we must have chartered a plane from Iona and that the only closed cabin plane in Ireland at that time was their de Havilland Fox Moth, a four-seater bi-plane. So apparently that must be what we went in, to fly from Baldonnel to Croydon.

We knew nothing of air luggage, and our leather suit-cases and Gladstone bags occupied the other two seats of our little plane. In Croydon we boarded a relatively enormous Imperial Airways plane and flew to Cologne. There we said we wanted to go on to Frankfurt. So you want to be driven to the railway station? No, I said, we want to fly. Oh well, we must see what we can do for you. So they rustled up a small plane for us. Again, it was only big enough for ourselves and our luggage and in it we flew, as the sole passengers, to Frankfurt. I have no recollection of what happened after that, nor of the return journey, but we would not have been in such a hurry to get home, so no doubt we adopted a more generally accepted mode of travel. The whole journey was no great extravaganza. Our travel costs were paid out of the legacy of £75 each which we received as executors.

For the purposes of administration, Aunt Zinnie had appointed my father and me as executors of the 'English' part of her estate and we conducted a considerable amount of bilingual correspondence, an interesting experience for me, with the district court in Königstein, our lawyers, shipping agents and others, over the next two years.

At the Three Candles, we had a bookshop in the front of our premises. Our main business was supplying the county libraries, with which Colm was well connected through his lectures to the School of Librarianship in UCD. For most of my time at the Three Candles, the bookshop was in charge of a native Irish speaker from County Mayo, Mícheál Ó Rodaigh, who would always speak to me in Irish and would always start with the words, *'Cogar anois anseo'*, that is, 'Whisper here now'.

It was not part of my regular duty to deal with customers' initial enquiries; but it happened that one day in April 1940 I was in the shop when Bea Orpen came in. I did not know her, not having seen or heard of her since childhood; but I was happy to talk to her. She enquired about the possibility of doing design work for us, but I was not able to give her any encouragement, as we had our own design staff and never went outside them. We also talked about doing a series of Christmas cards, which in fact we did print for her some months later. I saw her to the door and watched her walking up Fleet Street. After a short distance she turned and smiled at me. That day I told a close friend of mine that I had met the girl I wanted to marry. We were married approximately three months later.

Curiously enough, although the marriage took place in County Dublin, in Tullow Church, Carrickmines, close to the Orpen family home, the date had to be fixed for a time when there was no spring tide in Killybegs, County Donegal. This strange fact arose because,

Bea Orpen, crayon drawing by Seán O'Sullivan, 1940

Photo: Des Clinton, Drogheda

Bea's father having died in 1939 and her brother being on active service with the British navy, she was to be given away by her brother-in-law, Hugh Delap, who was married to her sister, Kathleen. Hugh was a civil engineer with the Office of Public Works and was engaged in engineering works in Killybegs harbour. He had to carry out inspections at spring tides. Otherwise he could take a day off. He always carried a book of tide tables in his pocket, and thus he fixed the date as 5 July 1940.

The Emergency, as the war years were known, made it impossible to see any future in the printing business, not only because there was less commercial work to be done, but also because of the difficulty of obtaining raw materials, principally paper, a bulky product that had to be carried in what few ships were still coming into Irish ports with merchandise. So, in March 1941, when things looked particularly bleak, Colm gave notice to the whole staff and took back on a temporary basis those for whom work could be found. He wrote me as nice a letter as he could in the circumstances, telling me of his decision and giving me a month's notice.

I was at the time actively involved in the first ever Irish Book Fair. It was organized by the Friends of the Irish Academy of Letters and the Dublin booksellers, and I was a member of the committee as one of two representatives of the Irish branch of the Associated Booksellers of Great Britain and Ireland. It was held in the Mansion House, and we had a very impressive list of speakers at the various functions. They included Lord Longford, Denis Johnston, Lennox Robinson, P.S. O'Hegarty, Edmund Curtis, M.J. MacManus, Lynn Doyle, Alice Curtayne, An Seabhac, Earnán de Blaghd, Riobárd O Farachain, Austin Clarke, Patricia Lynch, Winifred Letts, Elizabeth Bowen, Maurice Walsh and Colm O Lochlainn.

I worked out my month at the Three Candles and left. By then I had a wife and child, our son, Fiachra, but as luck would have it I was not very long out of a job.

Details of the operation of 'The Three Candles in the 'Thirties' are to be found in an article under that title which I have contributed to *Long Room: Ireland's Journal for the History of the Book,* No. 41, 1996, published by the Friends of the Library, Trinity College Dublin.

Wedding Day, 5 July 1940

Photo: J. Ross, Dublin

X

Youth Hostels

A German experience which had a major effect on my life, and on the life of other people in Ireland too, was the discovery of the *Jugendherbergen* and my acquaintance with them, first with Dr Sander's school and then on my visit to Heidelberg and on my later cycle tour down the Rhine. I recorded my experiences with much enthusiasm, including the fact that my hosteller's card cost me five pence and my overnight fee twopence (50 and 20 Reichspfennige respectively).

Two years later, in Cambridge, I learned that a Youth Hostels Association of Great Britain, as it was first called, had been established, and I heard that it was planned to extend the organization to Ireland. I was disturbed by this, as I felt that it was important for its success that any such organization should spring from Irish roots.

The President of the YHA was the Professor of Modern History in Cambridge, Dr G.M. Trevelyan, an enthusiastic cross-country walker. Early in 1931 I went to see him and he told me that my information about the YHA extending its activities to Ireland was incorrect and he gave me every encouragement to establish our own organization.

I wrote home to my father and asked him to set up a meeting during the Easter vacation in April 1931 where I might talk with some representative people with a view to starting youth hostels in Ireland. My father made some contacts for me and a small meeting was held at Grianblah, our family home, attended by representatives of the scouts and other outdoor organizations.

The attendance included Thekla Beere, at that time a statistician in the Department of Industry and Commerce, who later became Secretary of the Department of Transport and Power, the only woman to reach such heights in the Irish civil service.

I had to go back to Cambridge for my finals, and in my absence, on 7 May 1931, a general meeting was held in University College, Dublin, in Newman House, and at that meeting An Óige actually came into existence. An organizing committee of nine persons was elected, which included Thekla Beere, myself and also Colm O Lochlainn.

At this meeting Colm produced the name 'An Óige'. That was a stroke of genius, as otherwise it might have become Cumann Brúanna Óige Éireann or something equally clumsy and unlikely to have gone around the world as the name of An Óige has.

So An Óige was born, with its primary object formalized somewhat later as: 'To help all, but especially young people, to a love and appreciation of the countryside, particularly by providing simple accommodation for them in their travels'.

The committee lost no time in getting down to the job of opening youth hostels. They were originally for the use of walkers and cyclists only, though they have for many years been open to all comers. With no funds other than a score of five shilling subscriptions, they had a hostel of sorts open in a barn at Loch Dan, in County Wicklow, within three weeks of that May meeting. This was for men only — 'men of the Early Heroic Age', as Marion Lavery, a prominent member in the early days of An Óige, called them. I was of that number, one of the few who actually slept at Loch Dan.

As soon as I had come down from Cambridge, I took up the position of Honorary Secretary of An Óige and plunged into the work of developing a youth hostel chain. Loch Dan was followed by two cottages, for men and women, at Laragh and two more at Glencree, this latter forming a happy relationship with the Oblate Fathers in Glencree as long as they were in that glen. It was natural that for the first few years the activity of An Óige should be concentrated on County Wicklow, because of its accessibility from Dublin, which was clearly the major market for the services which we had to offer.

However, from a very early date I set about establishing contacts with people in other parts of Ireland who might be interested in the youth hostel idea. It was a particular pleasure to learn that there were people in Belfast who would like to meet our committee.

In November 1931, a group of seven or eight persons from the North came down and walked with a like number of us from Dublin to the cottages in Glencree, to spend the night there. The immediate outcome of the discussions held there was the establishment of a Northern Branch of the association, which then became known as the Irish Youth Hostel Association (An Óige and Northern Branch).

The Northern Branch had complete autonomy in the six north-eastern counties and was linked with An Óige through the person of the Honorary National Secretary, (a title which was first held by myself). The Northern Branch had by Easter 1932 opened three hostels in County Down, but it became clear that in order to obtain badly needed public support they would have to form a separate Youth Hostel Association of Northern Ireland. This was done in September 1932.

Though this was a great disappointment to me, we have maintained cordial relations with our sister organization in the North ever since and had close co-operation in particular in joint publicity and other matters of common concern.

In 1934, with a view to making a link with the northern hostels, we opened our first hostel north of Dublin, namely at Mellifont, in County Louth. The building, within the walls of the old abbey, was the property of Mrs Balfour, of Townley Hall, whom I visited on an introduction from my father. He was a cousin of Mr Balfour, who had died in 1926. Mrs Balfour let us have the building on very favourable terms, and on her demise it was donated to us in 1957 by its new owner, Mr D.G. Crichton. Come the 1990s it was no longer possible to mantain the hostel to the standards required. The building was sold to the Office of Public Works, who in 1996 re-opened it as an exhibition centre for visitors to Mellifont Abbey.

When we first acquired the building it was basically in good order. This was not a usual experience. The rented houses and cottages which made up the five hostels in County Wicklow had mostly been in bad repair. It was a feature of the early years that members of An Óige gave their work voluntarily to mend roofs, lay floors, build chimneys, glaze windows, make and hang new doors and construct all the furniture — transforming damp and dilapidated cottages into dry, cheerful hostels.

Many young people, particularly those who from an early age became involved in work parties and committees, made a most important contribution to the development of the organization and were able in later years to look back to their time with An Óige as by far their most rewarding experience.

From the very beginning of An Óige's existence, I was keenly interested in the international aspects of the youth hostel movement and as early as 1932, I had negotiated reciprocal arrangements with YHAs in England and Wales, Scotland, Denmark, Switzerland, Belgium, France and Norway. Germany had great problems in those years of depression and had difficulties about making reciprocal arrangements. As a sign of gratitude for their having started the whole movement, we agreed to accept German hostellers in our hostels without reciprocity.

Having made our existence known abroad, even in our infancy, we were invited by the Netherlands Association to send two delegates to the first International Youth Hostel Conference, to be held in Amsterdam in October 1932.

There was a certain amount of scepticism about our participating in such a conference. What had we to offer? How could we have the temerity to stand up and be counted with our three hostels against Germany's 2,200, Switzerland's 178, England's 134? And there were of course no funds to pay delegates' expenses, but I was determined to go and Colm O Lochlainn agreed to go with me. So we did go and, being represented there, An Óige became a founder member of the International Youth Hostel Federation and was actively involved in all subsequent conferences.

There was a total of twenty-two delegates at that first conference, representing eleven countries, and the business was conducted entirely in German. Ireland was largely unknown on the

The first International Youth Hostel Conference, 1932. From left to right: Bernasconi and Binder (Switzerland), Catchpool (England) (standing), Solum and Ouren (Norway), Bolman (Netherlands), Simon (Sudetenland – Czechoslovakia) (standing), Miss Krebs and Pedersen (Denmark), Ó Lochlainn and Trench (Ireland), Miss Lander (England), Björnson-Langen (France) (standing), Miss Dambuyant and Sangnier jun. (France), De Combe (Belgium-Flanders), Meilink (Netherlands), Laban (Netherlands Minister of Education), Schirrmann (Germany), Deelan (Netherlands), Münker (Germany), Blonski and Orlowicz (Poland). *Photo: N.V. Polygoon, Amsterdam.*

European continent in 1932, and the delegates were surprised to hear Colm and me speaking Irish together. I have referred in an earlier chapter to the 'Common-Room Evening' at which Colm sang in both Irish and English and played the piano for my dancing of an Irish hornpipe and how this was for the Dutch and the other delegates their introduction to Irish music.

The international conferences were held each year in a different country and each year I planned my annual two-weeks vacation to coincide with the time and place of the conference.

That first conference was the most enjoyable of the seven which

I attended. With only twenty-two delegates, we got to know each other. There were no tensions, political or otherwise. Richard Schirrmann, founder of the youth hostels movement in Germany, presided. He made friends with us all and we were all devoted to his ideal of fostering *Das Wandern von Volk zu Volk* — youth hostelling from nation to nation.

In the following year, Colm O Lochlainn was again my fellow-delegate to the conference, this time in Germany, and what a change we saw from the Germany we both had known. The brown shirts were everywhere, even on the German delegates to the conference. It was the least well organized conference I was at, with transport breakdowns and overloaded programmes, some of which had to be abandoned. And the tension was palpable and increased over the next years as the Nazis tried to gain control of the conferences and to oust Schirrmann.

I was in England for the third international conference in 1934. The Economic War was in full vigour at the time, imposed on Ireland by the UK government following de Valera's announcement, on taking office in 1932, that he would not transmit to the UK the land annuities accruing from tenant-purchasers under the Irish Land Acts. I felt strongly that the UK action was unjustified and as a matter of principle I did not accept the invitation for the delegates to visit No.10 Downing Street, but went straight to the conference centre in Derbyshire. So I missed drinking tea with Ishbel MacDonald, who received the delegates in the absence of her father, Ramsay MacDonald.

The conference was still quite small, twenty-eight delegates representing fifteen associations. I had issued a general invitation to the delegates to visit Ireland after the conference. There was competition from Scotland for the post-conference tour, so it was gratifying that nine of the continental delegates chose to come to Ireland. They came from Belgium (Flanders), Danzig, Germany, the Netherlands and Switzerland and included the president and secretary of the International Federation, Richard Schirrmann (Germany) and H.L.F.J. Deelen (Netherlands).

They were given private accommodation in Dublin, Schirrmann

staying with me. He needed an interpreter as he had not a word of any language other than German.

In two days our visitors visited all An Óige's hostels — Mellifont in County Louth, and four in County Wicklow. They had a ten-minute chat with Éamon de Valera in his office in Government Buildings. They may have known virtually nothing of Ireland, but they had certainly heard of de Valera. They were presented to him by Colm O Lochlainn, who would have been known to him personally. That was my first meeting with de Valera and it was the delegates' first reception by any Prime Minister.

They had an evening's entertainment in the apartment of Raghnal de Brún (or Ronald Brown) where the programme included Irish songs by Colm O Lochlainn and Máire Ní Shéadha, who played the harp, and dances by Jimmy Ennis, accompanied on the uileann pipes by his son Séamus and on the piano by Michael Bowles. Subsequent conferences took me to Poland and Czechoslovakia, Denmark, France and Belgium, and Switzerland. My fellow-delegate for the first two of these conferences was Ruth Childers and for the last two Phyllis Thompson. They were prominent members of the Publicity and Hostels Mangement Committees of An Óige. It was a great thrill for me to represent Ireland at all these conferences and I was proud to be able to demonstrate that we were not dependent on the English language for communication with the outside world. German continued to be the official language of the conferences, without translation, and all my public utterances were in that language except when I spoke in French at a Youth Rally in 1937 at the Foyer de la Paix de Bierville, Boissy-la-Rivière (Seine-et-Oise) to introduce my singing of *Is truagh gan mise i Sasana*, which I had learnt from Colm O Lochlainn's sister, Una, and its translation into English by Thomas MacDonagh, one of the executed poets of the 1916 Rising.

The last conference before World War II was held in 1938 in Switzerland, and I was invited to speak at it, together with a Flemish delegate, on the subject *Die Jugendherberge im Dienste volkstümlicher Bewegungen*, which might be translated 'Youth Hostels in the service of national cultural movements'. This invitation arose from the known interest of the Flemings and of myself in, to quote the second

With Queen Beatrix of the Netherlands and Dr. Eric Ketelaar, chairman of the Netherlands Youth Hostels Association, at the Golden Jubilee Conference of the International Youth Hostels Federation, in Noordwijkerhout, August 1982

Photo: N.V. Polygoon, Amsterdam

object of An Óige, the fostering of an appreciation of our 'cultural and historic heritage', including language and music, song and dance. The treatment of the subject was particularly appreciated by those who represented ethnic minorities who felt their cultural heritage to be under threat from their stronger and more numerous neighbours.

For Ireland to be represented at international conferences in the 1930s was by no means the everyday occurrence it has become since the 1960s and 1970s. My attendance at these seven conferences entailed what was for those days an unusual amount of foreign travel. I felt that I was in this respect highly privileged. It was of course entirely at my own expense and I could afford this because I was living with my father, to whom I was not expected to make any contribution, and my salary rose to £3 and then to £5 and eventually to £7 per week!

Even at this level of pay I could afford to buy a car, by hire-purchase. My first was a 'Baby' Ford, i.e. 8 HP. I bought the chassis in 1936 and had a very sporty open body built for it, the like of which was seldom seen. This enabled me for instance to dash off for a weekend to Donegal or Tipperary to secure the gift or loan of a house suitable for conversion into a youth hostel (Trá na Rosann in 1937, Mountain Lodge in 1939) or to help with a work-party on the rebuilding of the old schoolhouse at Baltyboys.

After eleven years as the Honorary National Secretary of An Óige, I resigned from this position on leaving Dublin in 1942; but I remained on the National Council from its establishment in 1943 and never completely lost touch. I wrote a detailed account of the origins and growth of An Óige for the association's Jubilee, *Fifty Years Young: The Story of An Óige,* published by An Óige in 1981.

In the following year, I was a special guest of the International Youth Hostel Federation for its Jubilee Conference in Amsterdam and Noordwijkerhout. I was thought to be the sole survivor of the first conference, held in Amsterdam in 1932. I was certainly the youngest, but very belatedly, just before the Jubilee Conference was about to open, Margot Krebs-Dollerup, in Denmark, was discovered. She had attended the first five conferences, and had very efficiently organized the conference in Copenhagen in 1936; but immediately after that, she went to South America, where she remained for some forty years, working in Chile for Justice and Peace, and she had lost contact with Herbergs-Ringen, the Danish Youth Hostels Association.

Queen Beatrix of the Netherlands addressed one session of the conference at Noordwijkerhout. I was presented to her, I have a nice picture of her laughing at something I said, though what it was I do not remember.

An Óige had by this time become one of the largest voluntary organizations in Ireland. At its peak it had over 30,000 members, and fifty-five hostels in sixteen counties. It had been built up on an immense amount of voluntary work, manual as well as administrative, and it had come to be regarded as one of the great successes of the age.

With An Taoiseach, Dr Garret FitzGerald and Liam Lambert, President, An Óige, at a function in the Gresham Hotel, Dublin, when Dr FitzGerald was presented with honorary Life Membership of An Óige, April 1985

Its contribution to the truly world-wide youth hostel movement, in spite of its relatively small size, was recognized by the election of its Honorary National Secretary, and later President, John Bourke, as First Vice-President of the International Federation for six consecutive years.

I am happy to have been associated with this organization in its infancy, and I confess to being pleased when strangers still want to shake my hand and thank me for having introduced into Ireland a movement which, as its historians have noted, for the first time enabled young people of modest means to enjoy the natural and cultural heritage of their own and other countries and to meet the youth of the world.

XI

Paddy

My brother and I were never very close. In fact we were not a close-knit family at all, neither as between the siblings nor between us and our parents — very unlike the Orpen family. Apart from myself, there was nobody whose company Bea enjoyed more than that of her own sisters.

The distance between Paddy and me in earlier years was largely a matter of age and of the different educational establishments which we attended. While I was at Repton, Paddy was firstly in TCD but he did not complete his course there and went instead to the Dublin Metropolitan School of Art. He had already been remarked on as a painter when he was at St Columba's College where the art master was Richard Caulfeild Orpen, RHA, an Old Columban and a distinguished architect and watercolourist and a consummate draughtsman. He was the eldest of four brothers, of whom the second was Bea's father, Charles St George Orpen, and the youngest was (Sir) William Orpen, RA. Cerise Parker, Bea's eldest sister, remembered a conversation with her Uncle Richard, at Carrickmines station, when he told her that he had a very interesting new pupil at St Columba's, one Patrick Trench, who loved painting on a large scale.

The artist, Hilda van Stockum, writing in *The Irish Times* of 23 March 1985 on the 'Dublin Art School in the 1920s', remembers two students who 'kept rather apart from the main stream of the art school; their names were Salkeld and Patrick Trench. Patrick Trench was rather literary'. Other students whom she mentions as contemporaries of hers, and of Paddy's, are Maurice McGonigal, Seán O'Sullivan, Harry Kernoff, Nano Reid and Brigid O'Brien, all of whom became very well known in later years.

Patrick Tuohy, who had been a student of William Orpen's at the School of Art, had served with the Irish Citizen Army in the GPO in the 1916 Rising, and was now a teacher in the School of Art. He was one whom Paddy particularly remembered, although Tuohy left Dublin in 1927, after teaching there for nine years, and went to New York, where he died sudddenly in 1930.

Tuohy introduced Hilda van Stockum to the Radical Club, where she met poets and other writers, such as Fred Higgins, Séamus O'Sullivan, Liam O'Flaherty and Francis Stuart. Paddy was there too, though not apparently contributing anything to the violent arguments of the men of letters.

I knew, or at least met, all these artists and the writers, in later years. I remember Paddy saying that Kernoff told him that when travelling in Central Europe and the USSR the only language he needed, to get around anywhere, was Yiddish. Kernoff had a Russian Jewish father and a Spanish Jewish mother.

My sister, Shamrock, would have met some of these people too, in particular the painter, Cecil Salkeld. He had a cottage in Glencree, where Paddy was convinced he intended to seduce Shamrock. Paddy went out to him and told him that he had a gun and would shoot him if he laid hands on her.

Shamrock was very attractive to men. One whom she captivated was the surgeon and author, Oliver St John Gogarty, who used to drive her out to Baldonnel airfield in his Rolls Royce and arranged for her to get flying lessons with the Irish Aero Club of which he was a founder member. He told her that if she continued she could become the first woman in Ireland to get her pilot's certificate for solo flying and Lady Heath would then give her a scholarship, to enable her to train as a professsional pilot.

Father very reluctantly paid for the requisite number of flying lessons. He regarded Shamrock as a dangerous car driver and could not imagine what she would be like in an aeroplane. He had a series of second-hand cars, which he changed fairly frequently. They all had open tops with the sole exception of a Baby Austin saloon, which did not last long. He was very generous as far as I was concerned, letting me drive the car even before I was of an age to have a licence (one could take chances then that one would not take now), and letting me take it off on my own whenever he was not actually using it. But as for Shamrock, he had a device in at least one car, the Lea Francis, which enabled him, if sitting beside Shamrock when she was driving, to cut off the fuel suply with his toe without her knowing. In those days the petrol tank was in front, directly over the engine, so it was not unusual for the fuel pipe to come down by the front passenger's feet, where it could have a tap on it. However, Shamrock did in fact pass her flying test, and was the first woman in Ireland to do so. But that was the end of that. There was no Lady Heath scholarship to pay for any further training and Shamrock felt that she had been badly let down by Gogarty.

In 1926, Paddy, aged twenty-one, married Frances Cautley Baker. Francie's mother was an Englishwoman, an artist, who had married, secondly, a medical doctor, Francis Kennedy Cahill, with consulting rooms and residence at 80 Merrion Square, Dublin. I had an idea that Mrs Cahill had promoted this marriage as a good catch for Frances. I believe that she wanted to make Paddy into a socialite and that she got a dinner-jacket suit made for him. I doubt if he ever wore it. I bought it from him for £1 and got it altered down to fit me. (Paddy was six foot four inches in height.) It is the only dinner-jacket I have ever had and it is stilll in use when occasion demands. The Kennedy Cahills entertained lavishly and regaled their guests with music after dinner, reviving in the 1920s a long tradition of private entertaining in pre-Great War Dublin.

Frances was deformed by very severe curvature of the spine, which gave her a hunch-back. She had been to the leading coeducational boarding-school in England, Bedales, where she had had a very bad time. The other children were really nasty to her and mocked her for being a cripple. Her mother founded the Crock of Gold, a shop whose windows, as George O'Brien recalled, were always full of gaily coloured tweeds and homespuns and together with the Sod of Turf tea-rooms and P.S. O'Hegarty's Irish Bookshop, all in Dawson Street, had a pleasant atmosphere about them, being 'in the Ruskin–Morris tradition of arts and crafts, of the intelligentsia redeeming the vulgarity of trade'.

I do not know what Father thought about the marriage; but he probably agreed with Mother who was unhappy about it from the start as she considered Francie 'inadequate' for Paddy.

After their marriage they went to Vienna, where Paddy attended Art School and whence he came back with tuberculosis. He had contracted TB some years previously and had had glands cut out of his neck.

We were living at this time in Balnagowan, Palmerston Park, and Father converted the stables into a dwelling for the newly-weds and called it Tawnabeg. I do not know what he intended that to mean, though I think I remember him saying that it meant a small *trench*! I cannot find how it could mean that. *Tamhnach bheag* would be a small grassy field on a hillside, which is scarcely appropriate! They hardly lived there at all. Paddy spent some time in a sanatorium in Switzerland, in Davos.

Francie had a sister, Lettice, a photographer, married to a man named Ramsey, and living in Cambridge, where I dined with them once early in my time there. They were involved in left-wing politics to some extent. Father strongly disapproved of Lettice, as he had an idea that she was trying to persuade, and indeed was successful in persuading, Paddy to desert Francie and go off with another woman and that she regarded this as an interesting sociological experiment. That would have been in 1928 or 1929, when Paddy did in fact go off with Evelyn Hayden and moved to London. He did not return to Ireland until after Father's death in 1939.

His marriage with Francie was dissolved in 1930 and in that year he married Eve. In that year also, Francie married an older man, Michael Farrell, author of an immense and complex autobiographical novel, *Thy Tears Might Cease*, written in the 1930s and published in 1963, after his death, with a lengthy introduction by Monk Gibbon.

As is clear from his novel, Michael hated his family background of small town shopkeepers and he felt that he was entering a higher social class by marrying Francie. He helped her with the management of the Crock of Gold, but neither of them had any business sense. They lived happily together until he died, in 1962. His place in the Crock of Gold was then taken by his elder brother Seán, a widower, who had run his own business and now put the Crock of Gold properly on its feet. It became very profitable and was eventually taken over by Seán's two sons.

Francie's mind failed her in her last years and having made few friends in her life, she was now cared for devotedly by her brother-in-law, Seán, and his sons and their wives. When she eventually had to be moved to a nursing home for constant minding, they continued to look after her and visit her. Francie died in 1982. I had met her only once over a period of some fifty years. I happened to sit beside her at a meeting in the Royal Hibernian Hotel. It had to do with industrial design and with exporting, in both of which I was interested. On the other side of Francie sat Seán, whom I did not know, and it amused her to introduce us as 'My brother-in-law, Seán Farrell — my brother-in-law, Terry Trench.'

During my three years at Cambridge I visited Paddy and his second wife, Eve, a few times. They were married on 24 November 1930, which was as soon as possible after the divorce from Frances came through. I stayed with them one night in what was probably the worst accommodation they had. It was in Old Gloucester Street, WCl, near Holborn. Paddy had a dramatic story, no doubt exaggerated, of how word would be passed along the street when the army of bed-bugs was on the march. Paddy and I went out to a pub near the British Museum, which was a short distance away, and met a few friends of his, one of whom was Barbara Nicholson, a young artist with whom Paddy worked on a big mural in the Holborn swimming baths and who became a medical illustrator and later an illustrator of botanical books for the Oxford University Press and ecological charts for the British Museum. Paddy and Barbara lived together for about a year and they had a daughter, Jane.

Some ten years after Paddy and Eve were married, he told me that at a time when he was seriously ill with TB, Eve had appeared on the scene and had nursed him with great care and devotion. He was convinced that she had saved his life and that he would always feel under an obligation to her. He recalled that as Mother was dying (she died on 3 February 1930) she said that he must be sure of a home with Eve. He was then legally married to Frances and considering Mother's ideas on the subject, that was going a long way indeed and was very generous of her. Father too, in spite of the distress which the whole situation caused him, was generous in trying to help them. He had in fact already in January 1930 bought a small house for them — 'Burretts', near Headley, in Hampshire. I stayed with them there too, when Pat, the first of their two daughters, was a small baby, and heard Paddy addressed as 'Captain', as it was assumed that every likely looking man around there was, or had been, an army officer. The place was about ten miles south of Aldershot.

It must have been extremely distasteful for Paddy to have always been dependent on his father for financial support; but it was very fortunate for all concerned that such support was forthcoming. Paddy had a brilliant brain, but he could never make a living for himself. In more favourable circumstances he might well have made a living as an artist, or a writer, or a scientist, but he was constantly hampered by tuberculosis. He also produced a film script in October 1939, which I showed to Eddie Toner and Liam O'Leary, directors of the Irish Film Society, of which I was a member. They were very interested, but nothing came of this.

Father died in July 1939, and when war broke out in September, Paddy and Winifred, who was later to become his third wife, came over to Ireland and tried to get a small market garden going, firstly at Balscadden, on the steep slope of Howth Head, and later at the Strawberry Beds, Chapelizod, on the steep slopes of the River Liffey, but what with drought and rabbits, nothing worked out right for him. He took up the study of zoology in TCD and worked as a laboratory assistant in the zoology department there under Prof. James Brontë Gatenby. He did some quite important work as he discovered a hitherto unrecorded sponge in the Liffey. I remember him being particularly concerned about moulds. He was also interested in wasps and told me something of the fascinating story of their social organization, as described by the French entomologist, J.H. Fabre.

Paddy had been out of Ireland for ten years and he did not much care for renewing his acquaintance with old friends. Cecil Salkeld he found to be 'over-fatted and a complete bore', Geoffrey Coulter 'a depressing person, poor chap'. So for light relief he turned to re-reading Hegel, Marx's *Capital,* and *The Positive Outcome of Philosophy* by Joseph Dietzgen, the Elder, a German who had developed the theory of dialectical materialism independently of Marx.

XII

An Irish Trotskyist

After I had come down from Cambridge, in 193l, I was almost never in England except in transit to or from the Continent. Consequently I seldom saw Paddy during those years and I was not in touch with his activities. Politically, I knew that he was a communist, but I never knew what sort of communist he was nor how active he was, until I started researches many years after his death.

It was as a member of the Independent Labour Party that he met Winifred Stidolph, who was secretary to Fenner Brockway, 1927 –29, in his capacity as editor of *The New Leader*, the ILP weekly. She was also secretary of the ILP Guild, a federation of dramatic societies

In 1936 civil war broke out in Spain and Paddy went to Spain, as a non-combatant journalist attached to POUM *(Partido Obrero de Unificacion Marxisti)*, the Workers' Party of Marxist Unification. George Orwell was similarly a member of the ILP and associated with POUM. This was a socialist party, a sister party to the ILP, both being affiliated to the International Bureau for Revolutionary Socialist Unions, for which the ILP provided the secretariat from August 1935. As the civil war progressed, the Communist Party in Spain was responsible for very repressive measures against POUM, as well as against the Anarchists.

POUM was not Trotskyist but had some members who were influenced by Trotskyism. It was independent of the international communist movement and critical of the (Stalinist) Communist Party, advocating policies far to the left of that party. Its main strength was in Catalonia, where it was the most coherent and strongest group in the ranks of labour.

I understand that Paddy wrote from Barcelona, anonymously or pseudonymously, for *The New Leader*, of which Brockway was editor 1926–29 and 1931–46, and for the *Bulletin* of the Trostykist faction of the ILP.

The New Leader has reports from 'Our Own Correspondent' in Madrid 1935–36. He is in Paris in July/August 1936, in touch with POUM leaders. John McNair, General Secretary of the ILP and author of 'In Spain Now' (ILP pamphlet 1936/17, Sept. 1936, 16pp) and other pamphlets, is named as the representative in Spain of the International Bureau and the ILP, organizing medical and other aid in Barcelona, for which funds were raised by the ILP, and reporting to *The New Leader*. 'Our Own Correspondent' reports from Barcelona on 4 December 1936. If this was Paddy's only contribution, it seems small indeed, but he may also have been feeding information direct to Brockway, who writes frequently on the Spanish situation, and whose pamphlet, 'The Truth about Barcelona' (ILP pamphlet 1937/2) declares, in an advertisement, that the best socialist reports from Spain appear in *The New Leader*.

Paddy did some paintings in Barcelona, but the only one I ever saw is very small. It is, however, interesting because it shows the streets beflagged with the Republican colours. Possibly the beflagging refers to the occasion when the Fascist revolt of 17 July 1936 in Barcelona was defeated by the workers and the red flags of the CNT (Syndicalist Trade Union under Anarchist direction), the UGT (Syndicalist Trade Union) and POUM were raised on all the buildings as a symbol of possession (ref. Brockway, 'The Truth about Barcelona').

This picture of Paddy's is in the possession of Andrée Sheehy-Skeffington. She and her husband, Owen, lecturer in French in TCD, were very good friends of Paddy's when he was back in Ireland, in the 1940s, and he appointed Owen as executor of his Will, together with Winifred.

Winifred moved to New Zealand late in life, to join her daughter and four grandchildren there. They tell me that she had two small paintings done by Paddy in Spain, one a landscape and the other a self-portrait, with Paddy wearing 'his red Spanish Civil War hat'.

Paddy's activity in Spain came to an end when he was admitted into hospital in Barcelona with a recurrence of TB. He was discharged, or he discharged himself, before he was fit to travel. He recalled that he had been very ill indeed. There were considerable hardships on the homeward journey, and when he got back he was very weak and expected to die. He was persuaded by Eve to try for recovery in the countryside and to stay with her at Burretts. That was some time before the end of 1936.

Paddy was operating independently of those Irishmen who joined the International Brigade, but amongst his friends who went to fight in Spain, as well as the clergyman, Hilliard, of whom I have written at the end of chapter II was Geoffrey Coulter, also the son of a Church of Ireland clergyman. He was a member of the IRA and was assistant editor of *An Phoblacht* at a time when Frank Ryan was editor, about 1931–32, i.e. a few years before Ryan went to Spain, and Coulter too, as D.R. O'Connor Lysaght records.

Lysaght is the author of an article on the 'Early History of Irish Trotskyism' which was to form the basis of a chapter in a book on World Trotskyism by Prof. Robert Jackson Alexander of Stanford University, California. I quote from Lysaght at length because of what he says about Paddy.

With reference to the Spanish civil war, Lysaght, writing as a Trotskyist and trying to maintain an Irish heritage in Trotskyism, says:

> It was this that prepared the soil for Irish Trotskyism. It enabled a number of anti-imperialists to see the reality of Stalinite [here Lysaght inserts *sic*] practice outside Ireland. For the Stalinites did not seek to defend the Spanish Republic against Fascism alone. They were far more successful in defending its bourgeois government against the attempts of the Spanish workers and peasants to advance their own aims. This fact was recognised in particular by two Irish members of the Stalinite inclined International Brigade, Robert (Bob) Armstrong

> and Geoffrey Coulter and by an Irish recruit to the militia of the non-Stalinite Centrist P.O.U.M., Patrick Trench. Of all these the most immediately effective was Trench. He returned to Dublin and joined the Labour Party with the support of [Michael] Price (now Secretary of the Constituency Council), where he lectured on Marxism and published articles in the Constituency Council paper, the *Torch.*

Torch was the new four-page weekly organ of the Dublin Labour Party branches, and was well to the left of official party policy. Paddy contributed to it fairly regularly for some eighteen months from September 1939, the editor at that time being Cathal O'Shannon. Paddy's first articles made clear his viewpoint: we need the control of industry in order to guarantee fair wages and we need state power to guarantee that control; the slashing of real wages by the spectacular rise in prices since the outbreak of war was a deliberate and worked out international policy. He welcomed the 'Bloodless Revolution' whereby the Baltic states of Estonia, Latvia and Lithuania had now been liberated from Capitalism and added to the Soviet Union — 'whatever reservations one may have about the Stalinist bureaucracy', a tremendous step forward from the semi-feudal darkness of the Baltic lands with their 'strutting landed aristocrats.' (As a matter of historical fact, the landed aristocrats, like my friend Dina, had been driven out between 1919 and 1921 — nothing to do with the 'Bloodless Revolution' of 1939.) He urged that the question of Stalinism versus Trotskyism should be painstakingly and honestly studied by every individual and every section of the workers' movement. Is socialism possible in one country alone? Can fascism be defeated by an alliance between workers and the middle classes? On the subject of neutrality, he advocated the preparing of the workers for a state of revolt against any invader.

He wrote on Connolly, on co-operative farming, on turf production, on the seed scandal (private ownership of the grain and seed industries must go), on oatmeal profiteers and on a strike in the linen industry. His strongly socialist, Trotskyist, views caused some controversy in *Torch* and when he expressed surprise that this workers' paper should allow its columns to be used for what he somewhat exaggeratingly called fascist propaganda, the editor noted: '*Torch* thinks discussion is all to the good. Some intolerant critics even want us not to publish Patrick Trench.' That was in 1941. His last contribution to *Torch* was on 13 April 1941. Cathal O'Shannon, the reformist editor, says Lysaght, had been replaced in June 1940. By 1941 the left had lost control of Torch as the result of an internal putsch. It continued to appear for another three years.

According to Mike Milotte author of *Communism in Modern Ireland: The Pursuit of the Workers' Republic since 1916* (Dublin, 1984), *Torch* was 'without question one of the most popular and stimulating labour papers ever produced in Dublin, [and] contributed much to the phenomenal growth of the Labour Party in the city'. John de Courcy Ireland has said that it was Paddy who persuaded Price to start *Torch* in the first place.

Andrée Sheehy-Skeffington records that her husband, Owen joined a branch of the Labour Party 'recently formed by Patrick Trench and based in Pearse Street, conveniently close to TCD'. In November 1939 Paddy was secretary to the branch, his address being given as Balscadden, Howth, or c/o The Irish Seamen and Port Workers' Union. In that month also he enrolled Owen Sheehy-Skeffington as the fourth paid-up member.

Paddy, says Andrée,

> was an idealist socialist, anti-Stalinist almost to the point of Trotskyism. He had something of his father's thoughtful absent-mindedness, turned on politics rather than literature. Ideas poured out as impulses, raw and misshapen. An artist of talent, Paddy had absolutely no desire for recognition or money, and insisted on giving Owen a painting which Owen admired. He had gone to Spain at the beginning of the Civil War, and had mixed with anarchists in Barcelona... Owen was attracted by his philosophical turn of mind, and his non-combative approach even to the idea of class war. Membership remained small but the branch had quite an impact in the next three or four years... Owen believed the Labour Party to be aiming at a democratic socialist republic. Emergency conditions created by a European war made it imperative in 1939 that such a party be vigilant and active in protecting and defending the poorer sections of the community and initiating

progressive measures. He found many members fully committed to these aspirations among the rank and file of the party, particularly in the Pearse Street branch, whose membership was heterogeneous but keen.

Lysaght writes of Paddy's position in 1939:

As yet he was alone politically. Armstrong had gone to London, and Coulter, after contacting the Socialist Workers Party of America, dropped out of politics. However after its long delayed appearance, Irish Trotskyism was to be reinforced from two sources besides the Labour rank and file. [Some of the militant Republican movement] joined the Irish Labour Party and were won to the left wing by Price and Trench... In September 1939, when the Second World War began, members of an Independent British Trotskyist group, the Workers' International League, came to Ireland to establish a centre outside the British war-time repression... When the repression proved less draconian, most of the League returned to Britain. Bob Armstrong went to Belfast to build the left wing of the Republican Socialist Party there. Thomas Reilly [a Scot of Irish parentage] stayed to help Trench in Dublin.

John Byrne had gone to live in England in 1941 and had joined the Workers' International League. Lysaght says that by August 1948 he was one of only two Trotskyists left in Ireland, Paddy having died six months previously. In an unpublished interview given in 1987, Byrne referred to Paddy as 'an excellent comrade...an intellectual type of fellow', who did great work in the Labour Party. Jock Haston, one of the Trotskyists who had come over from Britain, 'used to go out to his place in Howth to hold discussions with him...the first thing [Paddy] formed was the Marxist Group. There were only a few people in it ...Bob Armstrong was friendly with Paddy and used to come down to see him and have discussions with him...a very fine comrade, very good, very deep and clear in his ideas. He did a lot of good work...and was well respected.'

Milotte notes that the Trotskyist movement attracted supporters in Ireland by its consistent anti-imperialism combined with anti-fascism. He, like Lysaght, writes from a Trotskyist point of view. However, though they won supporters, they could not recruit many of them as members, as fully-fledged Trotskyists. Their significance was, to put it in another way, that they were opposed not only to the fascism of the Axis, but to the imperialism of the Allies.

Lysaght continues:

> By 1941...there were two unofficial Trotskyist groups in Ireland, that in Belfast, in the Republican Socialist Party, and that in the Irish Labour Party in Dublin. Politically, they tended to differ on the national question... Armstrong...indeed, polemicised in the *Torch* against what he claimed was Trench's pandering to Nationalism. In the Labour Party, Trench's political struggles included demands for a sliding scale of wages, for more measures of nationalisation and against the removal, under clerical pressure, of the Workers' Republic as the party's constitutional aim... Trench's most persistent and most political fight concerned Irish neutrality. His stance on this reflects how far the position has degenerated in the last forty years... Trench (and Price) presented a conception of Irish neutrality as a positive war against the war. They urged that Irish Labour should use the twenty-six county state's position as a base from which to contact anti-Axis resistance movements and the anti-colonial movements in the lands of the democratic imperialists. In 1941, Trench persuaded the Labour Party Conference to pass a general motion on positive neutrality... The next year, however, a more detailed motion was defeated overwhelmingly.

The Minute Book of the Pearse Street Branch of the Irish Labour Party (NLI MS 15661) for 1942–44 records that P. Trench, Strawberry Beds, Lower Road, Chapelizod, and W. Trench of same address were admitted to membership in January 1940 and Paddy was a regular attender at weekly meetings from then until 10 February 1943 being Branch Secretary 1941–42. Winifred appears to have attended only two meetings, and these were after February 1943.

At the first meeting recorded in this book, 9 December 1942, Cde Trench 'speaking of his projected Left Wing Group, said...he thought he would be kicked out of the Party sooner or later, but it would be made clear that it would be on a socialist issue'. On 13 January 1943 he said that he wished to plan an attack on the reactionary leadership of the Administrative Council of the Labour Party and to give publicity to such Socialist measures (as given in Labour's Constructive Programme) as the Party was already committed to.

Owen Sheehy-Skeffington, who was also critical of the AC, was dismissed from the Labour Party in 1943, but I think Paddy may have been saved from expulsion by the fact that the Pearse Street Branch was 'dispersed', ostensibly on the grounds that its members were non-resident in its area. It was the only branch to be dispersed on these grounds.

Milotte says that 'for a time, the Trostkyist paper, *Youth for Socialism (Socialist Appeal* after June 1941), was published in Dublin' and Paddy was very much involved in this. Paddy also contributed to *Fourth International,* the Journal of the American Socialist Workers Party, one of the senior sections of the Fourth International, as the international Trotskyist movement was called. This is significant, since it means that Paddy was formally recognized as representing Trotskyism in Ireland. Paddy's Trotskyism would have been covert, not necessarily known to members of the Labour Party. Trotsky had been murdered in 1940 on the order of Stalinists, and Trotskyists would not have been inclined to declare themselves. The issues of *Fourth International* for December 1942 and March 1943 give Paddy's 'Letters from Ireland', an excellent account of life in Ireland at that time.

All this left-wing activity in Dublin did not, of course, go unnoticed in the right-wing press. Prof. Alfred O'Rahilly, President of University College, Cork, 1943–54, conducted a witch-hunt in a series of articles in *The Standard* (Dublin). The issue of 28 January 1944, under the heading 'Labour Inquiry on Communist Penetration', reported as follows:

> The Fourth International (called Trotskyists)...came on the scene [in Ireland] at the conclusion of the Spanish civil war. Prior to September, 1939, four of its emissaries, who had belonged to the International Brigade, arrived in Dublin and proceeded forthwith, undisguised, to work their way into the councils of the Labour Party.
>
> With amazing speed they wormed themselves into the good graces of persons in the office of the *Torch,* organ of the Dublin Constituencies Council of the Party. The ground broken, three of the four went back whence they came and sent a man from Glasgow [Tom Reilly] to work with the Trinity College Irishman [Paddy!] they left behind...in a short time there were five representatives of the Fourth International on the Dublin Constituencies Council of the Party.

In *The Standard* of 11 February 1944, Capt. Peadar Cowan, a member of the executive of the Irish Labour Party, in a letter, denies the dominance in the Labour Party of the unnamed members or former members of the Communist Party of Ireland and the Fourth International. The editor of *The Standard* replies: 'Who owns *Torch*?... What responsibility had the Labour Party for *Torch* when John de Courcy Ireland, *alias* Peter McQuillan, etc., Patrick Trench and other fervent Communists were using its columns at will to preach the gospel?'

It is interesting to note that Irish intellectuals who had been brought up in the Protestant tradition were disproportionately represented in left wing politics. They included Hilliard, Coulter, Armstrong, and de Courcy Ireland, as well as Paddy.

XIII

Kilkenny

I was less than a month departed from the Sign of the Three Candles when I saw that the Irish Tourist Association was inviting applications for the post of Topographical Surveyor. I applied and was one of thirty-three surveyors appointed on 6 June 1942 at £3 10s per week, plus a subsistence allowance of £3 a week when working away from home.

The purpose of the ITA Topographical and General Survey was to collect and record full information concerning all items of interest throughout the Twenty-Six Counties, under the heads of scenery, antiquities, curiosities, recreation, sports, holiday facilities, resort and urban amenities — in fact everything that might require to be known, or would be of interest, to visitors or tourists from home or abroad.

The survey was to be systematically carried out parish by parish in one's allotted territory, and we were given a set of six different forms on which to record the information under each heading, the set to be completed for one parish before proceeding to the next one.

We were each supplied with a camera and were required to photograph all objects of importance, or to provide drawings of them. These included not only antiquities and buildings of imposing character, but also 'objects which may be regarded as "eyesores" or a blot on the landscape — such as very ugly buildings, derelict sites, advertising hoardings, etc.'

The only permitted mode of transport to and within each parish was one's own bicycle.

I suppose that it struck me at the time, as it certainly did later, that this was a splendidly imaginative undertaking by the ITA, in the midst of a World War, to seize the opportunity, that might never arise again, to record all the natural and man-made features of interest in the Irish countryside. It also reflected, for possibly the first time, the national cognizance of the eyesores which marred the countryside and which later planning acts did so much, not always successfully, to prevent. Dublin was not included in this particular survey, so I asked to be posted to County Kilkenny, because I had various friends there, such as the Butlers of Bennetsbridge, the Stopfords of Kilfera, and the Smithwicks of Kilkenny City. This was agreed and I was to start on 17 June.

Bea had a friend in Castlecomer, Connie Johnson, who was married to the manager of Castlecomer Collieries, and it was arranged that I should stay with them until I found more permanent accommodation for myself and Bea and Fiachra, then nine months old. I was to meet Connie in the Royal Hibernian Hotel, Dublin, and travel down with her to Castlecomer.

My longest standing connection with anyone in Kilkenny was with Hubert and Peggy Butler, of Bennetsbridge. Hubert had lived in Russia for a time, then in Yugaslovia for three years, working for the School of Slavonic Studies, so that he spoke Russian and Serbo-Croat fluently, as well as German. In 1938 he was in Vienna, doing voluntary work in the Quakers' International Relief Centre, with the commitment to help Austrian Jews to emigrate. There was a group of some two hundred Catholic and Protestant Christians of Jewish origin for whom he made strenuous efforts to secure entry permits to any country in the world, where they might form an agricultural community, but they were not accepted anywhere. So Hubert turned his attention to individual families, and to a small number for whom travel was arranged to Ireland.

Although Hubert had two homes in Ireland, his own family home in County Kilkenny and his wife's family home in County Monaghan, he had been out of Ireland so much that he was not in close touch with things in Ireland and he did not know what he should do with these people when they arrived in Ireland. For advice, he turned to a leading Quaker in England, Jack Catchpool. Jack happened to be Secretary of the Youth Hostels Association (England & Wales) and had met me at the first International Youth Hostel Conference and several times since. He advised Hubert to make contact with me, possibly with a view to putting a youth hostel at the disposal of the refugees. That is how I met Hubert, for whom and for whose wife Peggy and her mother, Mrs Guthrie, I soon developed a profound regard and affection.

On our first meeting, Hubert stayed with me for a night at Grianblah and we then drove up to Peggy's home at Annaghmakerrig, County Monaghan. I made many visits to that great early nineteenth - century house in the years that followed. It was the first place that I took Bea to for a weekend together, for Mrs G, as Peggy's mother was always called, was one of the people I most wanted to meet Bea. It was soon after that, in the garden of Annaghmakerrig, that we agreed to get married, so Mrs G was the first person to be told of our engagement. Her companion, 'Bunty', was the second. Mrs G always needed a companion as she had lost her sight suddenly some years previously. Bea and I continued to visit there when cars were off the road and we took the train to Newbliss and were driven the three miles to Annaghmakerrig in the pony trap.

Annaghmakerrig is now the Tyrone Guthrie Centre, left by Sir Tyrone Guthrie, Mrs G's only son, as a retreat where artists, writers and musicians from Ireland and abroad, can work in peace.

I also visited Hubert's family home, Maiden Hall, many times. On one occasion he told me to meet him at the bridge over the River Nore, at Bennetsbridge. We were invited to dine at Kilfera, the home of Nancy and Monty Stopford, a short distance upstream from there. Hubert proposed taking me there in a cot, the flat-bottomed punt-like boat of the Nore, propelled by a pole, while our dinner-jackets, *de rigueur* at that time, were sent round by car. It seemed a delightful way to go out to dinner and to visit that beautifully situated house, even though Hubert had to get out and push the boat through weeds or shallows from time to time

Kilfera is Cill Fhiachra, Church of St Fiachra (locally pronounced Fierach), and his holy well is still there in the grounds and is kept in good order. I visited Kilfera several times after my marriage, and it was there that our first child was conceived. Hence we named him Fiachra.

Saint Fiachra is, or was, known in Ireland less well than in France, where he is acknowledged as the patron saint of gardeners. There are at least two villages of Saint-Fiacre in Brittany. One near le Faouet has in the chapel an effigy of the saint holding a spade. He is always kept supplied with fresh flowers. The sixth-century saint is somewhat anachronistically dressed as a Dominican, with a black mantle over a white habit.

On our first continental holiday, in 1954, Bea was in the chapel making a painting of the saint, but giving him the features of our Fiachra, while I was sitting outside studying the first thing I had bought as soon as we drove into Brittany, namely *Le breton par l'image*, published in 1944 during the German occupation. A commercial traveller, coming out of the local bistro, pointed to the EIR plate on our car and, with a French intonation, enquired, *'Sinn Féiner?' 'Mais oui, certainement'*, I replied. *'Notre chef est en Irlande'*, he said. This was a reference to Yann Goulet, former Commander-in-Chief of the Breton Republican Army, who had retired to Ireland to escape the French and German authorities.

I found another village of Saint-Fiacre while driving through Champagne in 1990. Here the saint is depicted with charming incongruity, holding a watering-can.

From the Hôtel St. Fiacre in Paris a Monsieur Sauvage operated the first hackney carriages in 1640. A figure of the saint stood in a niche over his door and thus the cab was called a fiacre in France and Fiaker in Germany and elsewhere. I saw what may well have been the seventeenth-century Hôtel, with an empty niche over the door, as the only building in the Impasse St-Fiacre in Paris 4e, in 1982; but when I went back to look for it two years later, the whole Impasse had been demolished in the developments around the Centre Georges Pompidou.

These references to Saint Fiacre arise from my recounting my associations with County Kilkenny before going to work there in 1942. After a few days in Castlecomer thanks to Connie and Harold Johnson, I heard from Eileen Smithwick, who had been kindly working on our behalf, that she had found the ideal house for us. Our new abode was one half of Newpark Lodge, on the edge of Kilkenny City, the home of a single lady, Miss McCreery, living alone, who had been persuaded by Eileen that she should have tenants in the unoccupied half of the house. We were the first of a number of such tenants. It suited us perfectly. Next door was Newpark House, the home of Mrs Dove. This is now Newpark Hotel, with the manager living in Newpark Lodge.

I continued my topographical work from there, cycling forty miles a day and more in northern County Kilkenny. For many years afterwards I was amused to see my phraseology cropping up repeatedly in the tourist literature for the county.

I had been working away at this for about six weeks when I received a letter from a firm in Drogheda asking me to come and see them if I was still interested in the job about which I had enquired some four months previously.

That was when I lost my job at the Sign of the Three Candles, and told Ruth and Erskine Childers. Erskine was at that time Secretary to the Federation of Irish Manufacturers. Quite by chance, Ruth at that time had a call from a neighbour in Highfield Road, Vera O'Connell. Vera told Ruth that Brydon Hill, of Drogheda, had died suddenly of a heart attack. He was married to Vera's aunt, Violet, and he was the managing director of the family's long-established business, McCann & Hill Ltd., Oatmeal Millers and Merchants, Drogheda, The business depended entirely on him, and Violet and his two brothers were faced for the first time with having to appoint a manager and had no idea how they were going to do this.

'I have the man for you', says Ruth, 'Terry Trench is a manager; he'll manage anything.'

Thus it was that I applied for the job in a business of which I knew nothing. When later I met Richard Hill and he showed me round the mill and offered me the job of manager, at my asking price of £500 per annum, I discussed the situation with the people in ITA. They could not guarantee any future for me though they were very pleased with what I had been doing and they recommended that I accept what looked like a more permanent appointment.

So ended my brief but happy sojourn in Kilkenny.

XIV

Drogheda

As soon as possible after winding things up with Kilkenny and the ITA, Bea and I took the train to Drogheda, with our bicycles, to search for a place to live.

We knew nobody, but Bea's mother had given us an introduction to Mrs Cairnes, of Stameen, whom she knew through their mutual membership of a committee of the Mothers' Union and through this introduction we were able to make a successful application for the tenancy on a caretaker basis of the premises known as the Blue School.

The original Drogheda Blue School, in the close of St Peter's Church, was established in 1723 for the education of sons of aldermen of the town of Drogheda. This curiously restrictive charity became meaningless during the course of the nineteenth century, and in 1865 Thomas Plunket Cairnes, a philanthropically minded brewer and landowner, had the terms of the Blue School Trust extended and a new building erected at the top of St Peter's Place. With the establishment of a National School under Church of Ireland management (its building was another Cairnes benefaction), there was little use for the Blue School and it ended up by being, perhaps uniquely in Ireland, a boarding house for boys from the country wishing to attend the National School. By the time we arrived on the scene there were only two such boys left and the principal of the National School had been enjoying free accommodation in return for looking after these boys. It was decided to close the Blue School and to let the premises until such time as they might be required again by the Governors.

When we cycled out to the Cairnes family home at Stameen (it is now the Boyne Valley Hotel) to meet Mrs Cairnes and to tell her of our quest for a place to live, she immediately decided that we were the right people to be the first tenants of the Blue School. We were in luck, for the Governors were to meet the following day. In the absence of her husband, Col. Tom Cairnes, grandson of Thomas Plunket Cairnes, she was in the chair and the Governors agreed to accept our offer of £108 p.a., which we had ascertained from the outgoing teacher was what they were looking for.

It was some months before the Blue School would be ready for us, so Mrs Cairnes phoned Mrs Johnston of The Glen, Mornington, and more or less commanded her to take us in as paying guests as she had plenty of room and she should not be living alone for so much of the time in her big house. For my first week at McCann & Hill's I stayed at Stameen, in great comfort, paying Mrs Cairnes whatever I had agreed to pay Mrs Johnston. Bea and Fiachra then joined me and we all stayed at The Glen, two-and-a-half miles down the Boyne from Drogheda, and I cycled in and out every day.

Mrs Johnston's two children were away from home — Maureen at the start of her medical career, Roy at boarding school — and her husband, Senator Joseph Johnston, Fellow and Professor of Applied Economics at TCD, came down to The Glen every weekend and at vacation time and helped to keep us in touch with the world at large. We moved into the Blue School on 26 February 1943. The removal from Dublin included my car and I had to apply for a special permit to drive it from Terenure to Drogheda, as all private motoring was stopped from April 1942 and did not resume until December 1945. It was a strange experience driving through the city and especially out into the country, almost completely devoid of traffic except for the occasional horse-drawn vehicle. That was my second very sporty car, an Adler cabriolet, with front-wheel drive and torsion bar suspension, which were great novelties at the time. It cost me £225 and I had just finished paying for it when it was put off the road.

The Blue School was the perfect house for us. The rooms were well proportioned and big enough to take my desk and other large

Bea working on designs for the Pageant of St Patrick held at Drogheda, Slane and The Hill of Tara, Easter 1956

pieces of furniture which had come to us from our parents and grandparents, as well as some large family portraits. The house formed the end of a cul-de-sac, so there was no passing traffic, and the garden was big enough for our children, in due course, and all the neighbours' children too, to play in, as well as having a kitchen garden where we employed a man once a week for a time to help us to produce all the fruit and vegetables we could and we let a neighbour have a plot there too. We became greatly attached to the Blue School which we often referred to as the nicest house in Drogheda.

I was interested to be working in an industry producing essential foodstuffs, principally flake oatmeal (or porridge oats) and wheatmeal (stoneground wholemeal) and basic animal feeds.

We were the second largest wheatmeal millers and the largest oatmeal millers in the Republic, with customers in every one of the twenty-six counties, if only we could get to them and produce enough to give them a fair share of what was available. Whatever quantity we could produce was never enough, and we could sell without any effort on our part. Our problems were those of securing raw materials from local growers, or, when this became possible, from Canada or Australia, and of distribution.

I also had to deal with labour problems, but these caused little trouble. A big difference from the Three Candles was that there we had a labour force at the top of the wages scale; in milling, we were near the bottom of the scale. As I have related in an earlier chapter, I did manage to establish better relations than had existed before, and I was pleased when my efforts culminated in my being addressed in a letter from one of the unions as 'Dear Comrade'. This happened accidentally, however and the secretary thought it necessary to come and apologize!

I worked long hours during the harvest and other busy seasons and otherwise normal office hours, but always found time for activities which were rewarding in other ways. I was very soon invited onto the committee of the Drogheda Grammar School which had been closed by the Erasmus Smith Board and recently re-opened by a local committee as a co-educational school. The first headmaster in my day was Fleming Thomson, who was quite a good musician, and organized and conducted a public performance of Handel's *Messiah* in which Bea and I took part. It was given in the Abbey Cinema by the Drogheda United Choirs in aid of the Lourdes and Cottage Hospitals in Drogheda. Staff changes at the Grammar School were rather frequent but Bea, as art teacher, survived to become the longest serving teacher in any subject.

In July 1945 I founded the Drogheda Branch of the Irish Film Society and ran it for three years. Unlike some other provincial film societies, we had the advantage of a full-size cinema screen, as our shows were always 'midnight matinees' in the Abbey Cinema, that is to say, starting at 10.30 p.m. after the last public showing.

Opening of Feis na Bóinne children's art exhibition, June 1960

The Blue School, Drogheda, the author's home 1942-60

In our first season we showed films from France, Britain, Russia, Hungary, USA and Austria, with shorts from Sweden, USA, India, Poland, Scotland, and England. At the end of the season I sent out a questionnaire to our members to ascertain their degree of satisfaction *(57%)* and their order of preference. Fourth in preference was *Hortobagy,* a beautiful and sensitive record of life on the plains of Hungary, with thousands of horses moving across the plains. However one member described it as 'for the most part a gross insult'. We could only assume that this was because it showed a foal being born, and possibly the antecedent to that, though I do not remember.

A second season included films from Russia, Switzerland, Denmark, France and Germany, and shorts from Britain and Canada, including francophone Canada. Our membership reached about one hundred and sixty; but with the removal of travel restrictions and the greater availability of good films from Europe in some of the Dublin cinemas, our numbers declined and we wound up the branch, feeling that we had done a good job but that our services were no longer required.

While this was going on, I was also, in 1946, a founder member of the Rotary Club of Drogheda. Rotary has not always had a good press and has been the target of cynicism from ill-informed quarters. To me it was of considerable interest and enjoyment. Bea and I did virtually no socializing. We did not play bridge, golf or tennis, but Rotary gave me an opportunity to find out what the business and professional men of Drogheda were interested in besides 'buying sardines in the cheapest market and selling in the dearest'. That was a phrase which I used at the first annual dinner, at which I was asked to reply to the toast of the Rotary Club of Drogheda. I could see that the president of the club did not like this. Perhaps he thought I was referring to him, but my choice of words was quite accidental.

Rotary gave me an opportunity to be of service, in a small way, under the four headings into which the Rotary principle of 'Service before self' was divided. I was the first to organize some Christmas entertainment for the inmates of the County Home. This was in the old Workhouse buildings, with two sections, one for geriatrics and the other for unmarried mothers and their children. We organized live entertainment in the wards and a film show and dance for the able-bodied, and I undertook the collection and distribution of toys for the children. We had all their names and ages, and Bea and I sat up late at night selecting the toys which we had received, and labelling them according to the age and sex of the child.

It was decided to give nylon stockings to the nurses. Nylons, I thought. Who wants nylons? I thought they were some cheap newfangled American gimmick, and that silk stockings were the proper thing to give to one's ladies. However, Bea assured me that nylons were all the rage and not at all to be despised! Thus it came about that, fifty years later, speaking at the Golden Jubilee Banquet of the Rotary Club of Drogheda, I was able to say, 'So this is for me the Golden Jubilee of the year in which I first discovered the charm of legs dressed in nylon.'

Our hospital visits were considered such a good idea that after a couple of years they were taken over by drama or other societies which were more specifically geared to that sort of thing.

My next suggestion in the medical sphere was that when the new mobile Blood Transfusion Service came to Drogheda and invited donors to attend at the White Horse Hotel, I sugggested that we should attend in a body. This was firmly turned down, one member saying that nobody was going to persuade him to be pricked by a nurse.

The general pattern of Rotary Clubs throughout the world is a weekly meeting for lunch followed by a fifteen/twenty minute talk by an invited guest on any subject of his or her choice. I was Speaker Finder for the Drogheda Club for about seventeen years and made many interesting contacts.

Amongst our most interesting visiting speakers were Lord Longford and Anew McMaster, each of whom visited us on two occasions when their respective theatre companies were on tour and came to the Whitworth Hall. Another was Miss Letitia Overend, Dame of the Order of St John and Chief Staff Officer of the St John Ambulance Brigade. She had been an ambulance driver in the First World War, and she drove a Rolls Royce open tourer, dating from that time I suppose, which she maintained and serviced entirely herself. She drove eight-year-old Brian in it back to the National School after his lunch break, which might have caused a sensation had he been observed.

I filled various offices in the club and was elected president for 1950–51. I see from the 1991 Roster that I was by that time the oldest surviving president of the club, my four predecessors, and several later ones, being listed as '(the late)'. In October 1950 one of our visiting speakers was Paul Millar, Chief of the Economic Co-operation Administration Special Mission to Ireland. That was part of what was otherwise known as the Marshall Plan. During the course of the lunch Mr Millar learnt that I was an oatmeal miller and that we, that is to say the McCann section of McCann & Hill, had been exporting oatmeal to the USA regularly since the 1830s and that this business had survived all the wars that had passed. I told him that the volume of business would not, unfortunately, justify a visit to the USA, at least not at present. He replied that they would pay our expenses if we made up a team representing the whole industry, not just my own firm, and that they would organize a Technical Assistance study tour for us so that we could see what was going on there.

At the next meeting of the Flake Oatmeal Millers Association I put forward the idea, which was immediately taken up and three agreed to go along with me — Senator Brian O'Rourke of Dundalk and Inniskeen, Co. Monaghan, R. Haskins of Wicklow and W. M. Scott of Omagh and Castlefin, Co. Donegal. All we had to pay was the return fare across the Atlantic. All other travel and accommodation was paid for by ECA. We sailed from Cobh on Cunard's m.v. *Mauretania*.

We had a very good three-week tour, first by train all night to Battle Creek, Michigan, and on to Chicago, where we were admitted to the trading floor of the Grain Exchange and business practically came to a standstill because everyone wanted to meet the Irish team. Another night journey took us to Minneapolis.This is not at all an Irish city, but rather Scandinavian.The telephone directory, for instance, starts with page after page of Andersen.

However, we were told that the night porter in our hotel would like to meet the Irish group before going off duty in the morning. So I went to speak to him. He may have been suspicious about my being Irish, not speaking with a recognizably Irish accent, and I could only slowly drag out of him that he was Irish, from the north, from County Monaghan, from 'a place you would never have heard of, called Inniskeen'. 'Did you ever hear of Barney O'Rourke ?' I asked. 'Did I ever hear of Barney O'Rourke? Sure, didn't his mother teach me my catechism?' 'Well that's Barney in there at the drugstore, having his breakfast.' I told Barney about this, and that disposed of him for the day. He had to go off with the porter and was not interested in visiting the Agriculture Department of the University of Minnesota, across the Mississippi, in St Paul.

In St Paul is also Hamline University, which Haskins and I went to visit because he had a cousin there who was Professor of History. Passing through the university library I took a quick flip through the card index and saw that they had nothing under the name Trench. When I got home I sent Prof. Rife a copy of my father's commentary on *Hamlet* and his little book on *Tom Moore* and some other items and in return he sent me *The Growth of the American Republic*, two volumes by Morison and Commager (OUP 1951), which he assured me represented the best in American scholarship, and to which I shall refer again shortly.

On Memorial Day, 30 May, to fill in time we were sent by air to Omaha, Nebraska, and by train thence to Cedar Rapids, Iowa, and on to Washington, D.C. (exactly one thousand miles in exactly twenty-four hours, with a two-hour stop in Chicago) and back to New York.

I was much the most junior of the team, in years and in status. The others were all virtual owners of their businesses. I was the only hired manager (but I had, by the way, been elected chairman of the Flake Oatmeal Millers Association before leaving home). I was also the most travelled, except for O'Rourke, and I was most *au fait* with what we were supposed to be doing and what the alternatives were when we had time to ourselves. I overheard O'Rourke saying, 'Only for Trench it would be bloody dull'. This became a sort of catch phrase and years afterwards when, on my way to Donegal one day I called to see Scott in Omagh, he greeted me with 'Only for Trench it would be bloody dull'!

O'Rourke was much the oldest of us, seventy-eight in fact. He could be quite entertaining talking about what it was like in the milling business in the early 1930s or before that. He was the only one of us who would have had the experience of taking the boat to Liverpool to buy, say, a small cargo of maize, perhaps four hundred tons to be shipped into Dundalk. We were dining in a restaurant one day and he was regaling us with stories about this sort of thing, haggling over half-a-crown in the price of maize when it was something like £5 a ton. A middle-aged couple at the next table, when they got up to leave, came over to us to say, 'Gee, it was so interesting listening to the old gentleman talking!'

After our official tour was over, I took an extra six days to meet our agent and to call on our principal customers, that is to say the leading high-class food stores in New York, Boston and Philadephia, where the white, black and gold tins of John McCann's Irish Oatmeal, still bearing the medals which McCann had won in London in 1851 and in Chicago in 1873, shone out from the shelves, quite distinct from anything else. The design was never changed and is still to be seen on those shelves, though from a different supplier since McCann & Hill went out of business.

That visit to America arose by chance out of having the right person sitting beside me as guest of the Rotary Club of Drogheda. When I became involved in the organizing of art exhibitions in Drogheda it was, again, my regular practice to have an official opening at 3 p.m. on a Monday and to invite the opener to speak to the Rotary Club lunch beforehand. Thus we had, for instance, in 1955 the Counsellor of the French Embassy to open an Exhibition of French Posters, and in 1959 the French Ambassador to open an Exhibition of Reproductions of Impressionist and Post-Impressionist Paintings, and the U.S. Ambassador to open an exhibition of Reproductions of Highlights of American Painting.

The US Ambassador was William H. Taft III, whom I had previously met as an official in the ECA Mission to Ireland. He was now on his first official visit to Drogheda and as I would be with him for some hours, and would be proposing a vote of thanks to him, I thought I should know something about his grandfather. However, I found that Morison & Commager's chapter on 'The Taft Administration 1909–1913' emphasizes 'the ineptitude of the administration', so I thought it best to pass that by.

One guest whom I specially invited to meet him was Alderman Laurence J. Walsh. Larry was mayor of Drogheda for fifteen years between 1934 and 1954 and was at the moment taking a year's (enforced) respite before becoming mayor again in 1956. He was particularly pleased to meet Mr Taft and to tell him that in any picture he ever saw of his grandfather's first public appearance at dinner in the Waldorf Astoria Hotel, the waiter standing behind his chair was Larry Walsh. Larry had in fact worked at McCann & Hill's before he took the boat to Liverpool to seek his fortune overseas. He worked on the building of the Panama Canal, and many of the steel plates with which it is lined bear the initials LW, for the plate-makers were required to identify themselves thus. In his years on the Council of the Corporation of Drogheda he was the only one who consistently expressed any interest in the efforts which Bea and I were making to set up a Drogheda Municipal Art Gallery.

In 1945 the Department of Education assembled a Loan Collection of Pictures by Irish Artists for Exhibition in Technical Schools. Bea was the art teacher in Drogheda Technical School on one night a week for thirty-one years from 1943 and she was asked to undertake the hanging of the pictures when they came to Drogheda. The collection consisted of one painting each by Sir John Lavery, Patrick Tuohy and Walter Osborne and fifty-eight of the best of our living artists from Jack Yeats and Evie Hone to Nano Reid and Bea Orpen, lent by the artists themselves for the purposes of this travelling exhibition.

I was asked to open the exhibition in Drogheda and I took the opportunity to suggest that the municipality should have an art gallery of its own. A public meeting was called and at my suggestion the Council of the Corporation was requested to appoint a Municipal Art Gallery and Museum Committee. This was done in June 1946. The committee comprised six extern members proposed by me, including Bea and myself, plus the Town Clerk, and seven members of the Council, to keep the balance! At the first meeting I was appointed Honorary Secretary and have continued in this capacity ever since, although the Committee has not met for some thirty years as the Council has failed to appoint a committee since October 1962.

When I was first appointed, the great question was where to find suitable premises and eventually we were given the front room in the Public Library building in Fair Street, which was not needed for the library. Bea and I immediately set to work to assemble both a permanent collection, by gifts, and a loan collection of works by Irish artists for our official opening. In this we had great support from our Honorary Art Adviser, R.R. ('Bobs') Figgis and from two distinguished artists who were natives of Drogheda, Nano Reid and most particularly Frances Kelly (Mrs F.H. Boland). We assembled twenty-seven works of art, some lent by the artists themselves, others borrowed from a number of private collections.

This exhibition covered roughly the same ground as the Technical School exhibition, namely from Nathaniel Hone to the present day, and it received unstinted praise from James White, the leading Dublin art critic. It went on for two months and was immediately followed by the public showing of twelve paintings which we had acquired as outright gifts and which formed the nucleus of the present permanent collection.

We held a wide variety of solo and group exhibitions in that front room, generally accompanied by a lecture, while our permanent collection, which was added to from time to time, was hung in the library rooms themselves. In October 1962 we were told that we could no longer have the front room as it was required for other purposes. That was the end of our temporary exhibitions.

The library itself was badly in need of new premises and year after year promises were made that it would acquire them and that there would be proper accommodation for the art collection. So we continued to accept gifts of paintings and to hang them in the library rooms until there was no room for more. In 1992 the foundations for a new municipal centre, to include the Drogheda Library, were laid. The pictures which had been hanging in the old library were renovated and restored by the Corporation of Drogheda, with assistance from Drogheda Chamber of Commerce, through the initiative of Austin Greene, and from the Bank of Ireland, and in 1994 the whole collection was rehung in the splendid new library.

It now consists of some sixty-six paintings and drawings which were, with few exceptions, assembled by Bea and myself over the years 1947 to 1981. They were nearly all donated by the artists or other benefactors, principally the Friends of the National Collections of Ireland, of which I have been a member since the 1930s and a Council member since 1955. Dr Michael Wynne, Keeper of the National Gallery of Ireland, visited the library in 1983 and in his report to the Corporation said that Drogheda was very fortunate to have such an interesting and varied collection of art works, many of them with a particular significance for the town and surrounding area, especially the two paintings attributed to Ricciardelli, which, he said, 'must be the envy of many another historic town'. These two eighteenth century views of Drogheda were already the property of the Corporation prior to 1947 and were added to the collection in the library at my request, along with three other paintings of local and historical interest. I compiled the Catalogue of the collection, with biographical notes on the fifty-two artists represented, and was very pleased with the end result, which was printed in Drogheda, with colour plates, and published by the Corporation.

My activities in Rotary and in the art world contributed to the interest and enjoyment of life; but up to 1965 I was still working full time at McCann & Hill's, the only interesting feature of which was that in the four years from 1956 our exports to the USA increased from $11,000 to $94,000. It was a tiny part of our business and would not have justified a journey to the USA if Córas Tráchtála (Irish Export Board) had not agreed to my request to sponsor the trip. We were virtually the only exporters of oatmeal from Ireland. A condition was that I should present them with a report on market conditions and prospects for oatmeal and oatmeal products in the USA and a confidential report on the distribution of McCann's Oatmeal. This was always pinhead (or steel-cut) oatmeal, quite different from Quaker Oats and other well-known brands.

In April 1960 I flew with Aer Lingus to New York. The flight from Shannon to Idlewild Airport in a Lockheed Super Constellation, leased from Seaboard World Airlines, took 14 hours. The Super Constellation was not jet-propelled; it had four turbo-charged piston engines.

Our most interesting customer was Catherine Clark and it was a pleasure to visit her in Oconomowoc, Wisconsin, a land of lakes and forests. Hers was a classic story of American enterprise. She was married to a bank official and had two daughters. When they grew up, she started baking bread in her own kitchen in the way her mother had taught her, and selling it to the neighbours. She then began to collect traditional bread recipes from different parts of the world and within ten years had a turnover of a million dollars. When I visited her she had a custom-built bakery with a hundred employees turning out 'home-made' bread on a large scale in many varieties, including an Irish Oatmeal Bread stated to be from a traditional Irish recipe. We were shipping the oatmeal to her in 50lb bags and her bread was so successful that enquiries came to us from some of the largest bakery chains in the USA. Catherine said she had no objection to our supplying them. They would never be able to compete with her 'home-baking'!

She opened a second bakery of her own on 'the coast', namely San Francisco, and she and her husband were living in happy retirement there, she having sold the whole business, when Bea and I visited them on our way out to Australia in 1974.

Before my 1960 trip we had already left the Blue School. That is to say that in June 1959 we had been given notice to quit because the principal of St Peter's National School was leaving to become principal of Taney School, Dundrum, which under his guidance became the largest Protestant national school in the Republic, and it was found impossible to replace him unless a residence were available. As the Board of Governors of the Blue School were largely the same people as were concerned with the national school, the simple solution to their problem was to give notice to the Trenches who were only there on a caretaker basis, albeit for sixteen years. This was a bitter blow to us. We searched everywhere for somewhere to live, but could find nothing. Eventually the Governors came up with their own idea for a temporary arrangement, which arose through their being also interested in the Drogheda Clergy Widows Trust.

Outside the gates of the Blue School were four rows of early eighteenth century alms houses, a total of sixteen houses, erected specifically for the widows of clergymen, but for over a hundred years they had not been all so occupied, for want of claimants, and all but a few were let to tenants whose rents helped to keep the roofs over the widows. No. 13 now became vacant and was offered to us on a quarterly tenancy at the rate of £50 p.a. Nine months had passed since we were first given notice to quit the Blue School and the Governors had continually pressed us to leave but had not actually thrown us out, so we felt obliged to accept the offer of no. 13. It was about a quarter of the size of the Blue School and had no garden, not even a patch on which our fourth child, Patrick, born in 1955, could erect his teepee. His playground was in and out of the graves in the adjoining church-yard.

I cannot now envisage how we managed to fit the four children in, when the older ones came home from college or boarding school. Fiachra was completing his first year at Trinity College Dublin; Brian and Beatrice were at Newtown School, Waterford. Looking through Bea's diary for that time, I do not find a single word of complaint or suggestion of any difficulty. She was wonderful at making the best of a bad situation. She continued to work a vegetable patch at the Blue School. We also retained for a time a room in which to store the furniture which we could not squeeze into no. 13, and another room which was Bea's studio, an essential feature of our economy.

In February 1961, in despair, we decided to look again at a house which we had viewed some months previously and had rejected. It was at that time occupied by short-term tenants who cared nothing for its appearance. The paper was hanging off the walls, the steps and balustrade to the hall-door were falling apart, the porch had collapsed, and in any case it was raining! On our second visit, it was empty. Bea immediately saw its possibilities, what each room would be and how the furniture would fit — and the sun was shining.

Next day I went into the agents and we bought the Old Rectory in Slane, County Meath, nine miles west of Drogheda, standing on one hectare, or two-and-a-half statute acres, for £1,750. And so, in June 1961 we moved finally from what had been a much loved house in Drogheda to what became an even more beloved house in the village of Slane.

XV

Slane

While I was living in Drogheda, with The Blue School as my address, it was natural that people should assume, as some indeed still do, that I was a schoolmaster. I did not want a similar mistake to arise when I moved to The Glebe, or The Old Rectory, in Slane. So I had it in mind that I must find a name which would be both Irish and meaningful and easily put into a form suitable for non-Irish speakers. I happened to come across the phrase *Grian na cille*. In everyday parlance, *grian* means sun; but there is also an archaic word *grian* which means land. So this phrase meant 'the land of the church'. This was exactly what I wanted, except that I decided that life was too short to have a house called Grian na Cille, with the constant necessity of spelling it and explaining it and how to pronounce it. So I made a composite word of it, thus, Cillghrian or Killrian. Before putting it into use I submitted it to Cearbhall Ó Dálaigh, whom I used to meet at Council meetings of the Friends of the National Collections of Ireland, and indeed had formerly met while walking in the Wicklow mountains. He was not only Chief Justice but a good Irish scholar. He approved of my composite word, after consultation with his wife, Máirín, a professional lexicographer, who was working on the Royal Irish Academy's *Dictionary of the Irish Language*. Thirteen years later, he became the fifth President of Ireland.

When I was living with my father and family in Palmerston

Park, our first house was Balnagowan, standing on five acres. After a few years, my father sold it, retaining one acre on which to build, in 1928, a smaller house, and one which would be more convenient for my mother, who was an invalid, and for whose benefit he turned it at an angle to get the maximum of sun. He too wanted to give it a name which would be correct in Irish. and suitable to the non-Irish speaker. He asked his friend, Douglas Hyde, Professor of Modern Irish in UCD, for the Irish word for sunflower. Dr Hyde gave him the name Grianblah *(Grian-bhláth)*. and ten years later, namely on 4 May 1938, was elected the first President of Ireland.

I continued to work in Drogheda for some years after moving to Slane and to keep up with some of my activities there. In 1963 I was elected President of the Chamber of Commerce for a two-year term, and in November of that year, on the day that John F. Kennedy was shot, I was making the final arrangements for the recently revived bi-Annual Dinner, for which I had secured the presence of An Taoiseach (Prime Minister), Seán Lemass, as guest of honour. The date arranged for the dinner was the date now announced for the Kennedy funeral, at which the Government

Killrain, Slane, the author's home since 1961. Drawing by Bea Orpen 1976

would be represented. Feeling in Ireland was so strong, that I found it necessary to phone Mr Lemass and ask him if he thought we should postpone the dinner and if another date would suit him. He immediately replied that if we postponed it for a few days he would come on the following Wednesday instead. There was no town in Ireland which had gained more than Drogheda from the Lemass policy for industrial development, so he was sure to be welcome whenever he came.

In my formal welcome to the guests at the dinner, I mentioned in particular a German guest, one of the first of a number of Germans who set up business in Drogheda. My words of welcome to him in German obviously pleased Lemass. Otherwise I had hardly spoken a word of German for over twenty years; but this position was to change dramatically.

The leading firm of milling engineers on the Continent was in Germany and they had a resident representative in Ireland, with whom I had never spoken a word of German; but on one of his visits he was accompanied by an older man, Georg Plange, who realized when we were looking at some promotional literature, that I could at least read German. He phoned me that night, asked if he might speak to me in German, and then asked me if I would consider changing my job. He was surprised at the readiness with which I replied in the affirmative; but for some time I had realized that there was no great future in oatmeal milling and that even if McCann & Hill survived through diversification, there would be no place for me, but only for the two sons of the late Brydon Hill, who were now in the business and could manage without me. So I had been on the look-out for possible alternatives.

Plange, who was in his sixties, had come to live in Ireland, having retired from active participation in the family business, one of the biggest manufacturers of flour and animal feeding stuffs in Germany. He was setting up a new import/export agency in Dublin, whose main concern to begin with would be to supply, on a brokerage basis, the raw materials for the manufacture of animal feeding-stuffs. If I was interested, he would like to see me at home. That was one of his ways of judging whom he was dealing with. So

Main Street, Slane. Drawing by Bea Orpen, 1976

he came to lunch at Killrian the folowing Saturday, we went for a walk along the Boyne, and he offered me a partnership in the business at a salary which would of course, he said, be more than whatever I was earning at the moment, and a share of the profits when we began to make any. I accepted and the Hills were glad to know that I had a good job to go to.

Plange's office was on the north side of St Stephen's Green and he had two German secretaries, who worked in shifts so that the office was open from 8 a.m.to 7 p.m. and Plange was there most of the time, early and late. It was a very interesting experience for me to be working in a modern office, for a change, equipped with photo-copier, in constant use, and telex, two novelties for me at that time.

I was in the office for less than three weeks, just getting on my feet, in May/June 1965, when I went off on a two-week tour to

London and Paris and Zurich and several places in Germany and Holland, to meet our likely suppliers, all of whom knew Plange personally or by name, and one of whom told me that he was well known to have fanciful ideas, which indeed proved to be the case. In November I had another trip to Hamburg and Amsterdam. As I was a prospective buyer, not a seller, I was well received everywhere, and I was pleased to find how easily I could conduct business in German and in French.

I was known to millers all over Ireland through the three millers' associations of which I was chairman (oatmeal, wheatmeal and maize), and through being a member of the Milling Advisory Committee, to which I had been appointed by the Minister for Industry and Commerce. They were our potential customers, but many of them were tied to existing sources of supply and it was difficult to break in. However, I did some quite successful deals; but Plange and I did not see eye to eye and we parted company after ten months. He had already taken another Irishman onto the staff, but the business did not last long after I left.

A few months later, at a meeting of the National Council of An Óige, it appeared to me that that organization was badly in need of a manager in the office. I offered my services and, as there was some doubt about this, I suggested a trial period of three months. This was accepted and I stayed for seven years. I had been warned privately by a friend of mine on the Council that I was letting myself in for a menial job, but I went ahead. And I did indeed learn how frustrating it can be for a professional to work for a voluntary committee, few of whom have any business experience. I would not have stuck it had I not been devoted to the ideals of An Óige. Eventually I gave a year's notice that I would stop work on my sixty-fourth birthday, by which time I would have qualified for a year's unemployment benefit, followed by a contributory old age pension for the rest of my life.

XVI

Retirement

As soon as I ceased to be an employee of An Óige, I was voted back on to the Council. I was elected President in January 1976 and in each year thereafter for six years, which was customary though not statutory. It happened that in the week after my election, Bea was elected National President of the Irish Countrywomen's Association, a position which she held for two years. Having the two presidents under one roof in the village of Slane caused some merriment and newspaper coverage.

During that time yet another president came to lunch with us, namely the President of Ireland, my old friend, Erskine Childers. He was on his way to open a *meitheal* (literally, a working party) at An Grianán, the residential adult education college of the ICA at Termonfeckin, on the far side of Drogheda. Bea was to preside, wearing her beautiful chain of office, which she had designed some fifteen years previously. She had been very much involved with An Grianán from its opening in 1954 and even before its official opening. Our lunch party at Killrian for the Childers visit, consisted of Erskine, his second wife, Rita, and his aide de camp, our neighbours the Marquis and Marchioness Conyngham, of Slane Castle, and Pic Mitchell, who lived at Townley Hall, near Drogheda. The dining-room table, with the red and gold crested dinner service, and the antique Waterford glass (making a very rare appearance) looked splendid and the lunch was prepared by Pic's adopted daughter, Rachel, a professional caterer.

The two presidents–of An Óige and of the Irish Countrywomen's Association–
Killrian, April 1975.

That was in September 1974. Exactly a month later Bea was to head a delegation of six members of the ICA (and three husbands) at the triennial conference of the Associated Country Women of the World, to be held in Perth, Western Australia. She had all her expenses paid, and I sold one book out of my library, namely Speed's Atlas of Great Britain and Ireland for £2,250, which enabled me to go with her. The best bargain we could make was to join a party of Women's Institute members from Britain on a Cook's Tour round the world. We went out by San Francisco, Tahiti and Sydney. We had three days in Tahiti and hired a car (very cheap!) to drive around the island on our own. It fascinated us because of its association with Paul Gauguin and we seemed to be seeing the figures from his paintings walking along the roads. Bea did some painting of her own there too.

For the opening ceremony of the conference in Perth the

leaders of the delegations from fifty-one nations had been asked to give a greeting to the assembly of fifteen hundred country women and three hundred husbands in not more than fifty words. Bea told me what she wanted to say and I composed it for her so as to make exactly fifty words, with particular reference to the Irishmen who had 'helped to shape Australia's history and here gained renown, supported by their womenfolk with indomitable courage'. Bea was resplendent in a long white báinín cloak, which she had bought as part of the 'trousseau' with which the ICA provided her. She was thereafter referred to as the Queen of Ireland. She always held herself so well, and regal indeed she looked.

Our world tour as originally planned was to bring us back via Bangkok, where we had hoped to meet up with Erskine Childers III, who was Director of the United Nations Development Support Communications Service there; but at the last moment we were told that we were being re-routed via Hong Kong, not Bangkok.

A few days before we left we chanced to have a visit from Sir Michael Hogan, formerly Chief Justice of Hong Kong. His sister, in the Medical Missionaries of Mary, Our Lady of Lourdes, Drogheda, was a friend of ours and a great admirer of Bea's. As a result of this visit, on our arrival in Hong Kong we were invited to lunch with Mr Horace Kadoorie. He had heard from Michael Hogan that we would like to get out of the city and into the country, so he arranged for his farm manager, Mr Woo, to pick us up at eight o'clock in the morning and to drive us out, about an hour and a half, to the Kadoorie farm. This farm, on a steep mountain side, was devoted entirely to the aid of subsistence and immigrant farmers, to enable them to become self-supporting by improving their husbandry and breeding healthier and more productive pigs and poultry. We saw the dramatic improvements which had been made in the shape and appearance of the Chinese pig and duck. These were given to those small farmers to help them to build up their own stocks of healthy animals. This was part of of the immense amount of philanthropic work in which the Kadoorie brothers, entrepreneurs of Iraqui Jewish origin, had been engaged.

After our farm visit, Mr Woo drove us to Government House,

where, thanks to Michael Hogan, we had been invited to lunch with the Governor, Sir Murray MacLehose, who had succeeded Sir David Trench, a second cousin of mine. The only other guests at lunch were a younger couple, a financial consultant from Tibet and his English wife. The Governor had been briefed as to what our interests were as far as Michael Hogan knew them — art, country women, youth hostels — and conversation flowed easily. After lunch we were driven back in the Governor's car, looked at with interest by passing motorists to make sure whether we were or were not the Governor and Lady MacLehose, back to our modest Chinese hotel in Kowloon. There was some surprise amongst the Women's Institute members that the two Irish Republicans were the only ones to be invited to Government House. Not least surprised was Delle Fletcher (née Chenevix Trench) who had lived in Hong Kong for some months while her husband was lecturing there on dendrochronology, on which he was one the three leading experts in the world — they had never been invited to Government House.

Three years later I accompanied Bea, now a member of the Council of the ACWW, to their conference in Nairobi, another memorable occasion, preceded for us by a three-day safari to the Samburu Reserve and Treetops, and followed by four days on the coast near Mombasa. Bea was kept busy at the conference, conscientiously attending all the sessions and being the principal speaker, with a talk on public speaking, at one of the study sessions; but she managed, as always, to get some painting done — at Treetops and in Nairobi and particularly on the coast, where we were on our own.

She was an artist of very considerable talent and there were people who thought that she was wasting her time with teaching and the ICA; but I could not agree. She loved teaching — she was a born teacher. She also loved her role as home-maker, and regarded the security of the home and her presence in it, as the most valuable contribution she could make to the well-being of our four children. She realized that she was very fortunate in being able to combine this with her profession as an artist and teacher. We were fortunate too in having a living-in domestic during most of the children's early childhood years. Those hours of teaching once a week in the Tech, the Grammar School and the national school, over a long number of years were important to her, because they meant that she got away from the house at those specified hours and nothing was allowed to interfere with that. She only gave up teaching when she became National President of the ICA. Under the Charlotte Shaw Bequest, administered by the Arts Council, Bea gave art appreciation talks to adult groups but particularly to schools all over the country. For this purpose she had large framed reproductions of paintings from primitives to modern times. She had a set of thirty-three, of the best quality available, selected by herself and provided by the Arts Council. She would take a few with her each time she went down the country to visit ICA guilds and she would always combine this with a visit to a local school, mostly national schools, and some in very remote places. Most of these children would have no pictures in their homes and would never have looked at pictures and I have seen them gape with wonder at what they were being shown and what they were being told. I was very seldom with Bea on such occasions; but she would often bring back entertaining stories of what had happened and remarks made. Things changed when television became commonplace and children were used to seeing pictures and to hearing the names of artists.

That set of thirty-three reproductions now hangs in Slane National School, presented at my request by the Arts Council as a memorial to her and in appreciation of her pioneer work in raising awareness of the visual arts. Each of the pictures is accompanied by a brief note written by me from what I knew her to have said about it.

One day in May 1978, she went to Dublin to deliver her usual quota of pictures for the Watercolour Society of Ireland exhibition and to attend an ICA meeting. She arrived home that evening with a splitting headache and looking very ill. The doctor came immediately and I drove her into hospital in Drogheda. She never came home again. She had in fact had a subarachnoid haemorrhage and had nevertheless driven herself home. In hospital she had a series of brain haemorrhages and became uncommunicative and, by degrees, quadraplegic. She partly recovered her speech but little else and she would look longingly at her hands, once so gifted, now lying helpless on the bedclothes. I tried to stimulate her with talk and with pictures. I had put Jan van Eyck's painting of the marriage of Giovanni Arnolfini on an easel beside her bed and she suddenly turned her head towards it. She nodded when I asked her if they (Arnolfini and his bride) had spoken to her. In what language? I asked. 'Italiano', she said and she gave a little laugh, for she spoke no Italian herself. I visited her every day for two years and two months, watching her gradually deteriorating. She died on 12 July 1980. By her stimulation of my interest in the arts, by her clear-sightedness and wise counsel, by her wit and humour, by her love and companionship, she had enormously enriched my life.

From the time of my retirement from full-time employment, I have enjoyed doing a certain amount of writing, mainly on subjects which required a good deal of research.

Early in my last year in the office of An Óige, Vivien Igoe, curator of the James Joyce Museum in the Martello Tower at Sandycove, asked me to give a talk in the tower on the following Bloomsday, 16 June. I protested that I was not a Joycean and knew nothing about Joyce. 'But you do know about Dermot Chenevix Trench', she said. Well, I didn't, but I supposed I could find out. This Trench, a third cousin of my father's, is generally accepted as the prototype of Haines, the Englishman in the tower in the opening pages of Joyce's *Ulysses*. I did the necessary research and managed to deliver what was regarded as an entertaining as well as informative talk, entertaining partly because I found fault with the pundits, including Richard Ellmann, the leading authority on Joyce. Vivien liked it and persuaded me to write it up and get it published.

As soon as I retired, I did some more research and made the talk into a more scholarly looking paper which was printed in the Fall 1975 number of the *James Joyce Quarterly*, published by the University of Tulsa, Oklahoma, and which Ellmann was kind enough to refer to as 'a very intelligent and useful piece of work'. I was amused to see in the notes on the contributors to this number, that all but one of the

In the ballroom, Slane Castle, for the launching by the Meath Association of An Taisce of *Slane,* written by C.E.F. Trench and illustrated by Bea Orpen. On right, Mr. Philip Mullally, Chairman of An Taisce, and, on left, Mrs. Eithne Olden, Chairman of the Meath Association, Nov. 1976. *Photo: Eugene J. Murphy, Drogheda.*

other contributors were professors or assistant professors of English in the universities of North America or Germany. My only distinction was 'B.A. in Modern Languages of Cambridge and Dublin, currently working on a book entitled *Slane: A Topographical Study'.*

So that was the next thing I worked at. *Slane* (without that sub-title) was a forty-eight page booklet, published in 1976 by An Taisce, the National Trust for Ireland, greatly enhanced by Bea's drawings. It was re-issued in 1987 with an extra sixteen pages of a *Slane Town Trail,* with ten more of Bea's drawings. Both editions were launched at receptions in the circular ballroom/library of

At Killary Harbour Youth Hostel, Co. Galway, July 1993, when HE Mary Robinson, President of Ireland, unveiled a plaque to commemmorate Ludwig Wittgenstein, who stayed in the building on this site in 1948 when completing his major work, *Philosophical Investigations.* On the President's left is Liam Lambert, past President of An Óige.

Photo: F. McMullan, Dublin

Slane Castle, possibly the finest Gothic revival room in Ireland, and which survived the disastrous fire which largely destroyed the Castle in 1991.

In 1785 Slane Castle had been substantially rebuilt, enlarged and altered by William Burton Conyngham and he was the subject of my next major piece of research. This research resulted in a lecture given in the castle to the Meath Archaeological and Historical Society, and in articles published in the journals of that society, of the Royal Society of Antiquaries of Ireland and of the Military History Society of Ireland. William Burton Conyngham was, amongst other things, an amateur archaeologist and I established, with some dificulty, that he was the first to receive permission to excavate the Roman circus at Tarragona, in Spain. This necessitated my going to Tarragona when I was in Barcelona for a short visit in 1986 and meeting the present Director of the Excavation of the Roman Circus, which is still going on after two hundred years. After my visit the Director sent me a copy of the *Diari de Tarragona*, with a front page banner headline, *Un Irlandès, el primer excavador del circ, l'any 1784* and a reference to myself as *historiador de la villa de Slane (pàtria de la família Conyngham)*. You do not need to have made a profound study of Catalan to understand that!

Research and writing continued to be a major occupation of mine, to keep my brain active in my septuagenarian and octogenarian years.

Now that I am coming to the end of my reminiscences, I look back to the most memorable event of the recent past, to the Bea Orpen Retrospective Exhibition. This was held in the Droichead Arts Centre, Drogheda, in June–July 1995. It was assembled by Hilary Pyle, and she compiled the catalogue with an Introduction about Bea's life and work, and an Appreciation by James White, former director of the National Gallery of Ireland.

The centrepiece of the exhibition was Seán O'Sullivan's portrait of Bea and round it were hung examples of her work from her student days to the last days of her life. It showed how she excelled in decorative design as well as in the gouache landscapes for which she was best known. The paintings were lent by public and private owners in many parts of Ireland, from Donegal to Cork, and the exhibition was formally opened by James White in the presence of all my family and many friends. The exhibition and the catalogue were a fitting tribute to the great treasure of my life.

In 1983 I visited my daughter, Beatrice, in Ottawa, my niece, Mary, in Toronto, and her daughter, Patricia, in Vancouver. Dining out in a Japanese restaurant, Patricia got me to talk about myself and the family and particularly about her grandfather, my brother, Paddy. She had a small tape recorder with her and she wanted to record all I was saying. Better still, she said. Why not write everything down, just the way you talk? And so I did.

80th birthday. The family presents the author with his portrait by Michael O'Dea, Nov. 1979

Photo: F. McMullen, Dublin.

Index

FROM THE BOOKPLATE OF
CHALMERS EDWARD FITZJOHN TRENCH
and BEATRICE ESTHER ORPEN

Other Titles from

THE HANNON PRESS

A LIFE BY THE BOYNE *by Jim Reynolds*

In his highly personal account of a life by the River Boyne, in Ireland, the author lashes out at those who have turned the magnificent river of his boyhood into a barren watercourse and through stupidity, arrogance and greed have destroyed the world renowned trout habitats at Lough Sheelin and Lough Ennel. A ZIRCON BOOK

TELLING TALES *by Eric Craigie*

Though earning a nickname for exaggeration as a child Eric Craigie maintained that "telling a story without a little trimming can often be dull". This delightful series of stories draws on his experiences as an industrialist, farmer, fisherman, crack shot and former Master of the Ward Union Hunt. A ZIRCON BOOK

AN IRISH SPORTING LIFE *by Eric Craigie*

Combining the best-selling *Irish Sporting Sketches* with *Telling Tales*, these sparkling memoirs by Eric Craigie, part history and part record of country life, warmly convey the humour and sorrows, and, above all, the unfailing celebration that have constituted his life as a sportsman. A ZIRCON BOOK *in Association with Lilliput Press.*

THE VIEW FROM THE CHAIR

The Art of Chairing Meetings *by Consuelo O'Connor*

Twenty-eight of Ireland's best-known names from the worlds of business, politics, the Roman Catholic church and voluntary sector play true confessions with Consuelo O'Connor about their own behaviour – and that of others – around the boardroom table. Fascinating for anyone who has to chair, or endure, meetings of any size.
Robert O'Byrne, *The Irish Times.* A ZIRCON BOOK

HOSTS & HOSTESSES

The Art of Irish Hospitality *by Consuelo O'Connor*

What is the most important ingredient in a successful party? Are black tie dinners out of date? Is Irish hospitality a myth? What is the protocol for a state dinner at Dublin Castle? Consuelo O'Connor gathers the experiences of well-known Irish men and women who reveal the secrets of their disasters as well as their successes.